100 Years of
The Souls of Black Folk:
A Celebration of
W. E. B. Du Bois

Robert Gooding-Williams
Dwight A. McBride
Guest Editors

D1518783

PUBLIC CULTURE

Society for Transnational Cultural Studies

PUBLIC CULTURE

Volume 17   Number 2   Spring 2005

100 Years of *The Souls of Black Folk*:
A Celebration of W. E. B. Du Bois

PUBLIC CULTURE

Society for Transnational Cultural Studies

Coming Attractions

Vol. 17, no. 3:
Jennifer Hasty examines the press in Ghana; Jason Frank on enthusiastic politics
and the public sphere; Jeffrey Lomonaco on Kant and model citizens; Elliott Colla
on Egyptian literary genres and the law; Jane Bennett on distributive agency;
Joseph Masco with a visual essay on nuclear activism; Lisa Kessler and Ann
Cvetkovich on the Catholic sex abuse scandal; and more . . .

Call for Contributions

mis·cel·la·ny, *n.:* a collection of various kinds, especially news clippings, literary extracts, postcards, and other images. Includes media accounts of items relevant to public discourse and debate throughout the world. The section seeks to highlight not only the reported phenomena as such but also the mediated nature of media coverage. *Public Culture* especially seeks pieces that are witty or (unintentionally) ironic. Submissions should include all relevant facts of publication and should be no longer than three pages.

et·y·mol·o·gies, *n., pl.:* true sense or form of the network of keywords: *public, publicity, public opinion, public sphere.* Investigates the contemporary uses and meanings of the terms *public, publicity,* and *public opinion.* Short essays (of approximately six to eight pages) that consider the semantics and pragmatics of one or more of these interrelated terms in the context of a particular language and a particular people are welcome. How do these terms compare across cultures and languages? Do their meanings "translate," and what do their "mistranslations" bode for comparative social theory grounded in what may be hidden ontological statements about civil society?

art·works, *n., pl.:* brief reports (up to 750 words) on innovative critical cultural work within and outside established institutions. Includes new kinds of museums; alternative or oral history projects; the expansion of musical performance and recording into forgotten musical histories or the dissemination of a broader range of musics; alternative publishing ventures or exhibition practices in film, theater, and dance; innovative cultural work with children; public art and art in public such as murals and graffiti; innovative uses of television, radio, or other mass media; and reports on past cultural work—the modernist, socialist, and avant-garde counterinstitutions of the early twentieth century. Send material and proposals to managing editor Plaegian Alexander.

from the field, *n., sing.:* briefly annotated single photographs for inclusion as a photo feature at the end of the issue. Submissions are not limited by style or content but should be glossy prints of at least 5" × 7".

CyberSalon: To join *Public Culture*'s on-line discussion group, send an e-mail message, "Add me to on-line discussion," to publicculture@newschool.edu.

Public Culture, New School University 80 Fifth Ave., Room 507, New York, NY 10011; tel. 212-229-5375; fax: 212-229-5929; e-mail: publicculture@newschool.edu; World Wide Web: www.newschool.edu/gf/publicculture.

100 Years of
The Souls of Black Folk:
A Celebration of
W. E. B. Du Bois

Robert Gooding-Williams
Dwight A. McBride
Guest Editors

Du Bois, Politics, Aesthetics: An Introduction

Robert Gooding-Williams

> *There is little evidence to suggest . . . that the methodology*
> *of formalism contravenes historical perspective or deep political*
> *commitment . . . a method is not inherently ahistorical, or endemic to*
> *a fixed, divine order. . . . The attempt, then, to treat a literary text by a black*
> *writer as a text (a spate of discourse operating according to certain formal*
> *principles) need not exclude the critic's whole consciousness,*
> *but, of necessity, draws its plenitude into specific concentration.*
> Hortense J. Spillers, "Formalism Comes to Harlem"

The essays collected in this issue celebrate the one hundredth anniversary of the publication of W. E. B. Du Bois's *The Souls of Black Folk*. Published in 1903 by A. C. McClurg, *Souls* is Du Bois's biting dissent from the racist and nationalist ideologies animating the public, political culture of post-Reconstruction, Jim Crow America. Announcing that "the problem of the Twentieth Century is the problem of the color-line," it is Du Bois's best-known attempt to explore the

Earlier versions of the essays collected in this volume were presented as part of "100 Years of *The Souls of Black Folk*: A Celebration," a conference honoring the centenary of the publication of *The Souls of Black Folk* and sponsored by the Alice Berline Kaplan Center for the Humanities and the Department of African American Studies at Northwestern University, October 24–25, 2003. For help in assembling this special issue of *Public Culture*, I thank the journal's editorial committee and especially Dilip Parameshwar Gaonkar, Beth Povinelli, and Claudio Lomnitz. I also thank Beth Povinelli, Claudio Lomnitz, and Dwight McBride for their very helpful comments on the first draft of this introduction. Thanks, too, to each of the contributors.

Public Culture 17(2): 203–15

"strange meaning of being black" in a society that was structured by racial apartheid and that consistently treated blacks with contempt.[1] To this end, *Souls* details a sweeping tableau of African American social and political life, highlighting the economic and social legacies of slavery, the fight for political and civil rights, and the contributions of African Americans to the spiritual and material formation of the American nation. The advent of *Souls* was an incisive event—an original, philosophically daring, and artfully wrought initiative that gave new life to the black resistance to white supremacy. In the words of David Levering Lewis, it "was like a fireworks going off in a cemetery . . . sound and light enlivening the inert and the despairing . . . an electrifying manifesto mobilizing people for bitter, prolonged struggle to win a place in history."[2]

Lewis's remarks could be taken as an epigraph for the volume as a whole, because they suggest that *Souls* is both a call to arms and an aesthetic event, at once a manifesto and electrifying sound and light—thus, a book that demands to be read equally as political argument and literary art. His remarks also resonate with the now commonplace claim that Du Bois's book invites appraisal from many disciplinary perspectives—including politics and literary criticism—because its impact and significance cannot be reduced to the terms available to just one such point of view. The essays collected here support this claim, for they demonstrate the possibility of combining literary critical analysis with detailed reflections on *Souls*'s larger political themes (e.g., white supremacy, homosocial patriarchy, and the relation between race and nation) to produce bifocal readings of *Souls*. Incorporating the sensibilities of the literary critic and the political theorist alike, they rely on the former to explore aspects of Du Bois's political agenda and on the latter to make sense of his aesthetic choices.

But these essays also support a stronger claim, namely, that the terms of literary criticism have a crucial role to play in exploring the efficacy with which texts establish their literary and political authority. More than any other instance of twentieth-century African American writing, *Souls* has emerged as an authoritative text: specifically, as a text that African Americans have regarded as establishing an appropriate discursive and normative framework for African American political and cultural practices. Few scholars would deny that Du Bois's critique

1. W. E. B. Du Bois, *The Souls of Black Folk*, ed. David Blight and Robert Gooding-Williams (Boston: Bedford, 1997), 34. All subsequent references to *The Souls of Black Folk* are to this edition.

2. David Levering Lewis, *W. E. B. Du Bois—Biography of a Race, 1868–1919* (New York: Holt, 1993), 227.

of Booker T. Washington addresses a constellation of political theoretical issues that have decisively (if not exclusively) shaped twentieth-century African American political debates—an eventuality that William Ferris seems to have anticipated when, just ten years after *Souls* first appeared, he dubbed it "the political Bible of the negro race."[3] And most would agree that *Souls* has played a decisive role in the formation of African American literature. Indeed, Arnold Rampersad has suggested that "all of African American literature of a creative nature" stems from *Souls*, while Henry Louis Gates Jr. has written that "no other text, save possibly the King James Bible, has had such a fundamental impact on the shaping of the African American literary tradition."[4] *Souls* has demonstrated an enduring efficacy as a source of both political and literary authority. As I argue below, it also conceptualizes these modes of authority as convergent, which is one reason why appreciating Du Bois's text as literary art is essential to appreciating its political influence. While *Souls* is historically rooted in the segregationist era of Jim Crow, it still demands our attention: the book's literary and political grip extends well beyond its origins, so much so that its compelling ideas and memorable themes continue to shape valuable discussions of black literature and racial politics in postsegregation America.[5]

Let me clarify the issues at stake here by distinguishing between *Souls* as a political theoretical defense of a politics and *Souls* as a performance of the politics it defends. As political theory, the book answers the question, "What kind of politics should African Americans conduct to counter white supremacy?" Thus it argues that a politics fit to respond to American racial apartheid must satisfy two conditions. The first relates to Du Bois's depiction of African Americans as

3. William H. Ferris, *The African Abroad; or, His Evolution in Western Civilization*, vol. 1 (New Haven, Conn.: Tuttle, Morehouse, and Taylor, 1913), 276.

4. See Arnold Rampersad, *The Art and Imagination of W. E. B. Du Bois* (New York: Schocken, 1990), 89; and Henry Louis Gates Jr., "Introduction," in *The Souls of Black Folk*, by W. E. B. Du Bois (New York: Bantam, 1989), xiv.

5. For a variety of recent examples, see Hazel V. Carby, *Race Men* (Cambridge, Mass.: Harvard University Press, 1998), 9–41; Gerald Early, ed., *Lure and Loathing: Essays on Race, Identity, and the Ambivalence of Assimilation* (New York: Viking Penguin, 1993); Kevin K. Gaines, *Uplifting the Race: Black Leadership, Politics, and Culture in the Twentieth Century* (Chapel Hill: University of North Carolina Press, 1996), 1–17; Henry Louis Gates Jr. and Cornel West, *The Future of the Race* (New York: Knopf, 1996); Paul Gilroy, *The Black Atlantic: Modernity and Double Consciousness* (Cambridge, Mass.: Harvard University Press, 1993); Joy James, *Transcending the Talented Tenth* (New York: Routledge, 1997); Adolph L. Reed Jr., *W. E. B. Du Bois and American Political Thought: Fabianism and the Color Line* (Oxford: Oxford University Press, 1997), especially chaps. 8 and 9 and the conclusion; and Daryl Michael Scott, *Contempt and Pity: Social Policy and the Image of the Damaged Black Psyche* (Chapel Hill: University of North Carolina Press, 1997).

"masses": to wit, to his characterization of African Americans as an aggregate of uncultured, premodern slaves, or former slaves. The second relates to his representation of black Americans as a "folk": that is, to his description of them as the bearers of a historically formed and collectively shared ethos, or spirit. For Du Bois, a politics suitable to counter Jim Crow had both to uplift the black masses—that is, assimilate them to the norms of modernity by battling prejudice and backwardness—and to articulate the ethos of the black folk. In short, it had to be a politics of modernizing "self-realization" (Du Bois's term) that expressed the spiritual identity of the folk: what I have called a "politics of expressive self-realization."[6] *Souls* enacts this politics—most explicitly, I think, in its concluding chapters—by presenting and distinguishing itself as an act of expressive and modernizing political leadership. Performing the politics it defends, the book is meant to satisfy the conditions it identifies as essential to a black American politics that would successfully respond to white supremacy.

As both theory and performance, *Souls* is a densely figurative and carefully plotted composition that invites literary criticism. In the essays belonging to the present issue, careful exegesis and nuanced interpretation underline *Souls*'s literary allusions, its iterated suturing of music and poetry, and its reliance on allegory and the aesthetics of the picturesque. Through readings that concentrate on what the epigraph to this introduction calls "formal principles," these essays engage Du Bois's book as political thought or political action while also offering insight into its success in establishing its authority. To be sure, not all the contributions echo, or obviously converge with, the reading of *Souls* I have sketched here (see, e.g., the essays by Alexander G. Weheliye and Vilashini Cooppan). Yet all of them raise questions bearing on *Souls*'s significance as political theory and political performance, and they do so by attending to its specificity as a text—to its use of allegory to understand the political significance of race, to its figurings of homosociality to conceptualize political leadership, and so forth. In a related vein, they also prompt the thought that the politics performed by a text, due to the literary complexity of that text, may quite unwittingly diverge from and put into question the theory the politics is intended to embody.[7] For most of the contributors to this issue, literary reading and political reading are inseparable.

6. Du Bois, *Souls*, 65. I present a similar sketch of *Souls*'s political philosophical argument in "Politics, Racial Solidarity, *Exodus!*" *Journal of Speculative Philosophy* 18 (2004): 118–28. I give a comprehensive and detailed reconstruction of that argument in my manuscript in progress, "Contributions to the Critique of White Supremacy: Du Bois and Douglass as Political Philosophers."

7. Here I mean to allude to the possibility of a more or less deconstructionist reading of *Souls*'s integration of political theory and political performance. I mean also to suggest that there is an affin-

Not all Du Bois scholars appreciate a critical consciousness that concentrates formal and other considerations. It is significant, for example, that the currently most influential study of Du Bois's political thought dismisses the idea that literary analysis can lend itself to political interpretation. Surveying the history of the critical reception of *Souls*, Adolph Reed has reproached petit bourgeois, postsegregation-era black intellectuals for giving short shrift to Du Bois's attack on Booker T. Washington and for preferring literary (or, more generally, "text-based") to political readings of the book. But Reed's polemic depends on two false premises: first, that Du Bois's response to Washington exhausts *Souls*'s worth as political thought; and second, that literary and political readings of *Souls* simply cannot coincide. As the essays here collected demonstrate, *Souls*'s importance as political thought far and away exceeds its treatment of Washington. As they also attest, the view that literary and political readings necessarily exclude each other, so that interpretation is always a matter of opting for one rather than the other, is not sustained by careful, attentive, and subtle readings of *Souls*'s political and literary strategies.[8]

The first essay in this centenary celebration is Cheryl A. Wall's "Resounding *Souls*: Du Bois and the African American Literary Tradition." Taking her bearing from Rampersad's suggestion that *Souls* is the ground from which all African American literature stems, Wall gives special attention to Du Bois's use of bars of music representing the sorrow songs as chapter epigraphs. Du Bois writes, she says, both as a historian and as a poet/preserver of the cultural memory the songs encode. Significantly, Wall describes *Souls*'s epigraphs as hieroglyphs that "withhold as much as they convey"—that is, as figures for the gaps in Du Bois's knowledge of "the history and experience of Africans in America."[9] In her view, African American writing in the wake of *Souls*—like Toni Morrison's *Song of Solomon* (1977), to which she devotes the second part of her essay—forms and

---

ity between some of the questions raised by the essays collected in this volume and those raised by Judith Butler's well-known and influential efforts to think the political and the performative in connection to each other. See, for example, *Gender Trouble: Feminism and the Subversion of Identity* (New York: Routledge, 1990) and *Bodies That Matter* (New York: Routledge, 1994).

8. Adolph Reed, *W. E. B. Du Bois and American Political Thought*, chap. 8. This chapter is an extended polemic against the literary criticism of Houston A. Baker Jr. and Henry Louis Gates Jr.

9. Cheryl A. Wall, "Resounding *Souls*: Du Bois and the African American Literary Tradition," in this issue.

extends the African American literary tradition through its effort to fill in the gaps left by *Souls*'s notable but finally incomplete poetic transcription of the "true," unwritten history to which the sorrow songs allude.

Very broadly speaking, Wall's analysis of the unfolding of African American literary history may be called romantic—provided that, in the spirit of M. H. Abrams, we think of romantic narratives as describing both the fragmenting dispersion of and the attempt to comprehend an original plenitude.[10] For Wall, that plenitude is the presence of an unwritten African American history and experience that *Souls* and subsequent additions to the canon aspire to articulate. But no individual articulation, not even *Souls* itself, fully captures and reveals that history and experience. According to the implicit logic of Wall's argument, every contribution to the African American literary tradition serves as a repository for a fragment of the extratextual plenitude that it incompletely communicates, even as it aims to advance the unifying telos of the tradition as a whole, which is to express and grasp that plenitude in all its richness.

Another implication of Wall's argument is that *Souls*'s aspiration to authenticity—that is, to give truthful expression to African American history and experience—has been the source of its literary authority. In other words, Wall suggests that African American writers have taken Du Bois's attempt to articulate accurately black Americans' history and experience as a fitting norm for subsequent African American literary productivity. Later writers have adhered to this norm, she suggests, precisely to the extent that they have followed Du Bois in pursuing the aim of authentic expressivity by, again, attempting to fill the gaps left by *Souls*'s achievement. Du Bois, arguably, would have been sympathetic to this implication of Wall's argument, for it agrees with his own account of *Souls*'s literary authority, which he links to its political authority. Thus *Souls*'s final chapters distinguish the music of the sorrow songs from that of debased "Negro melodies" (the "gospel," "coon," and "minstrel" songs) on the grounds that the former, but not the latter, afford authentic expression of the Negro folk-spirit.[11] Similarly, Du Bois distinguishes *Souls* itself from these debased genres by figuring his own voice, and the text it articulates, as an echo of the sorrow songs. For Du Bois, *Souls*'s literary authority converges with its political authority, for it is precisely *Souls*'s sympathetic articulation of the folk-spirit expressed in the folk song that,

10. M. H. Abrams, *Natural Supernaturalism: Tradition and Revolution in Romantic Literature* (New York: Norton, 1971).

11. Du Bois, *Souls*, 189. I develop this argument at greater length in chapter 4 of my manuscript in progress, "Contributions to the Critique of White Supremacy."

in his view, privileges the mode of political leadership he personifies through the act of writing *Souls*.[12]

If *Souls* succeeds in presenting itself as an authentic and authoritative text, that is in part because of the literary strategies it deploys. In "Du Bois and Art Theory: *The Souls of Black Folk* as a 'Total Work of Art,'" Anne E. Carroll discusses some of these strategies through a suggestive exploration of the possibility that Du Bois modeled *Souls* on Richard Wagner's idea of a *Gesamtkunstwerk*—a total artwork that succeeds in fusing poetry, music, and theater. Thus, Carroll's reading of *Souls* emphasizes the book's chapter-by-chapter epigraphic juxtapositions of European or American verse with bars of music drawn from the sorrow songs. In addition, her essay argues that while "Wagner was interested in creating an art form that reflected and called into being a unified German culture . . . Du Bois was concerned to do for African American culture—and, indeed, for American culture."[13] For Carroll, the Wagnerian Du Bois's synesthesia of song and poetry celebrates and shows the integrity of African American culture, even as it allegorizes and envisions the possibility of a racially integrated American culture.

Carroll's reading of Du Bois invites the thought that *Souls*'s efficacy in establishing itself as an authoritative text was in part a function of its affinities to *Gesamtkunstwerke*. Carroll notes that Du Bois wrote *Souls* to advance his antiracist political goals but worried that the book would not meet his aims for want of sufficient coherence and emotional impact. Du Bois addressed the first concern, she claims, by using *Souls*'s double epigraphs as thematic leitmotifs that also lend the book a visual and symbolic unity. He addressed the second, she suggests, by relying on the specifically musical epigraphs to affect the book's readers emotionally (leaving the poetic epigraphs to affect them intellectually) and to prompt them to actively engage the text—for example, to sound out mentally the printed notes they read. In Carroll's view, *Souls*'s impact as a critique of Jim Crow may have been due in part to the authority it acquired through its literary transmutation of aesthetic strategies that Du Bois discovered in Wagnerian opera.

As other critics have noted, Du Bois also drew on Wagner—and, specifically, on *Lohengrin*, which he later identified as his favorite opera—to frame the single piece of fiction appearing in *Souls*. In "Of the Coming of John," the protagonist John Jones serves Du Bois as a vehicle for analyzing the deficiencies of alienated

---

12. For a further development of this line of argument, see Robert Gooding-Williams, "Du Bois's Counter-Sublime," *Massachusetts Review* 35 (spring–summer 1994): 203–24.

13. Anne E. Carroll, "Du Bois and Art Theory: *The Souls of Black Folk* as a 'Total Work of Art,'" in this issue.

African American political leadership. Like Alexander Crummell (as Du Bois portrays him), Jones is a doubly alienated figure, an educated man of culture who finds himself equally estranged from both the racist whites who scorn him and the community of blacks for whose religiously inflected folk-spirit he has no appreciation.[14] Jones cannot be an effective black political leader, Du Bois implies, because he is oblivious to that spirit. But neither can he ally himself with similarly educated white men to bring about "a union of intelligence and sympathy across the color line" (Du Bois envisions "a few white men and a few black men of broad culture . . . joining their hands . . . and giving to this squabble of races a decent and dignified peace"), for white men view him with contempt.[15] Depicting Jones as a sort of tragic hero, Du Bois leaves him, at story's end, resigned to his double alienation and singing *Lohengrin*'s "The Song of the Bride" as he waits to be lynched.

In "Queering *The Souls of Black Folk*," the third essay collected in this issue, Charles I. Nero concentrates on Du Bois's treatment of John Jones's failure to ally himself with similarly educated white men—that is, on what Nero more precisely describes as Du Bois's lamentation on the inability of black men and white men to form a "patriarchal union . . . to establish a nation together." Considering Du Bois's tale from the perspective of queer literary theory, Nero argues that Du Bois's lament records his "anxieties" and " 'epistemological uncertainties' " relating to the "conceptions of normalcy" that governed "male bonding and the formation of patriarchal nationalism in the early twentieth century."[16]

At once literary and political, Nero's reading of "Of the Coming of John" shows how the "queer meanings" that qualify and organize the verbal and figurative texture of Du Bois's fiction imbue his patriarchal nationalism with homosocial desire and homosexual panic. Specifically, Nero argues that the story is a revision of "Jefferson Davis as a Representative of Civilization" (1890), the Harvard commencement address wherein Du Bois contrasted the Teutonic strong man to the black submissive man. In "Of the Coming of John," Du Bois reprises the figure of the submissive man in the character of John Jones. Noting that Jones identifies himself with the biblical Queen Esther and arguing that he assumes the feminine position of the bride when he sings Wagner's bridal song, Nero interprets Du Bois's hero as a figure for the frustrated desire of black men to establish homosocial, patriarchal bonds with white men. On Nero's reading, Jones's deci-

14. See Gooding-Willliams, "Du Bois's Counter-Sublime."
15. Du Bois, *Souls*, 147, 88.
16. Charles I. Nero, "Queering *The Souls of Black Folk*," in this issue.

sion to feminize himself expresses this desire but likewise incurs the risk of permanent feminization. Jones reacts to this risk with a homosexual panic that leads him to kill John Henderson, his white counterpart and the childhood friend whom the story figures as the specific object of his desire for homosocial union. After killing Henderson, Jones sings Wagner's bridal song to mourn the death of his beloved friend and to lament the impossibility of cementing homosocial political alliances between black and white men.

In "Du Bois and the Production of the Racial Picturesque," Sheila Lloyd pursues a similar theme by arguing that Du Bois invokes the tropes of literary romanticism—the aesthetics of the picturesque, in particular—to articulate his political desire to affiliate himself with *Souls*'s ideal reader, "a northern, educated, white man." Presupposing his estrangement from his ideal reader, Du Bois aspires to succeed where John Jones failed. In fine, he aims to annul that estrangement by eliciting his reader's sympathetic and critical interest in the "Negro Problem." Du Bois politicizes the picturesque by relying on its characteristically pictorial vocabulary to affect the sensibility of his reader—that is, to adapt his readers' perceptions to the landscape of the South in order that they may see and respond differently to what is observed there. Du Bois hopes to teach his readers to think critically by first compelling them to see and feel differently. Aiming to foster a shared sensibility and an imagination of community, he accords a place "to desire, affect, and the aesthetic . . . in the political project of querying and dismantling the color line."[17]

Notwithstanding the differences that distinguish their contributions to this volume, Wall, Carroll, Nero, and Lloyd all read *Souls* with respect to its salient racial or national preoccupations—that is, with respect to its interest in African American particularity or in the integration of African Americans into a more inclusive American polity. In "The Double Politics of Double Consciousness: Nationalism and Globalism in *The Souls of Black Folk*," Vilashini Cooppan productively expands this frame of reference by investigating Du Bois's attempt to think and politicize race, nation, and globe in relation to one another. Rejecting the received tendency to read Du Bois's intellectual career through the optic of a conversion narrative that finds in a "later" Du Bois a globalism, cosmopolitanism, or universalism that surpasses and repudiates the nationalism, racialism, or particularism of the "early" Du Bois—hence, the Du Bois who wrote *Souls*—Cooppan discovers in *Souls* "a distinct form of national and racial thinking that finds its expressive

17. Shiela Lloyd, "Du Bois and the Production of the Racial Picturesque," in this issue.

medium and its oppositional force in a certain kind of globalism." Rather than assert that Du Bois's globalism "succeeds, transcends, or sublates his nationalism," she holds "that it is only because he is one that he can also be the other."[18]

Cooppan claims that *Souls*'s distinct form of thinking yields a "new conceptualization and textualization of black identity." Combining the insights of Edward Said and Frederic Jameson, she defines this distinct form of thinking as "a contrapuntal or dialectical formalism that yokes opposites together at the scene of psychopolitical desire." Specifically, Cooppan argues that *Souls*'s contrapuntal formalism links and sutures race, nation, and globe: first, through a conceptualization of race as the "shattering source of division . . . within the nation and the redemptive site of memory, connection, and affiliation across the globe"; second, through a figuring of time "for which the psyche, with its recursive temporality of memory, at once backward-looking and forward-moving, provides a model"; and third, through the textual elaboration of "a certain literary figure, allegory, that is also characterized by a back-and-forth movement between two orders of time, space, and signification." Eschewing the thesis that race or, more concretely, black identity is a simple essence, Cooppan maintains that "race and nation, nation and globe are . . . not constituted 'before' or 'after,' 'inside' or outside' each other" but rather "in a mutually sustaining fluctuation between seemingly opposed yet secretly conjoined states of being."[19]

Near the conclusion to her essay, Cooppan writes that "*Souls* is a different kind of founding text. National in address, diasporic in its form, and marked throughout by processes of movement, be they those of migrancy, memory, or the allegory that is their textual double, *Souls* emerges as the kind of text that both grounds a tradition and keeps it moving." With these remarks, Cooppan invites an analysis of *Souls*'s foundational relation to African American literary history and of its circulation as an authoritative text that sharply contradicts Wall's analysis of these matters. Declining to posit the presence of a plenitude of history and experience that *Souls* but imperfectly communicates, Cooppan reads Du Bois as modeling an interpretation of black American identity as always exceeding the boundaries of the histories and experiences wherein we expect to situate it, for race and nation "expand, deterritorialize, and move."[20] *Souls*, for Cooppan, is what Gilles Deleuze and Félix Guattari might have dubbed a *conceptual rhizome*: a centerless map

18. Vilashini Cooppan , "The Double Politics of Double Consciousness: Nationalism and Globalism in *The Souls of Black Folk*," in this issue.

19. Cooppan, "Double Politics of Double Consciousness."

20. Cooppan, "Double Politics of Double Consciousness."

depicting lines of flight (trajectories of movement and deterritorialization, which she ties to migrancy, memory, and allegory) that persistently desediment and displace black identity, thereby preventing it from settling and congealing into the bounded, expressible plenary presence that Wall's romanticism seems to take for granted.[21] If *Souls* has succeeded in founding and keeping in motion a literary tradition, Cooppan suggests, it is not because its aspiration to authenticity has come to be regarded as a fitting norm for literary productivity but because its intratextual mapping of the movements that displace black identity have prompted still further displacements in writings that have drawn inspiration from *Souls*—as if, paradoxically, *Souls*'s displacement of black identity had been taken to have located a norm proper to the articulation of a distinctively black American literary sensibility; or, again, as if *Souls*'s public circulation as an authoritative text were a function of the impact on African American writers of its rhizomatic delineation of the circuits of black identity.[22]

In "The Grooves of Temporality," Alexander G. Weheliye sketches a reading of *Souls* that, no less forcefully than Cooppan's essay, puts into question Wall's romanticism. Like Carroll, Weheliye focuses on *Souls*'s chapter-by-chapter juxtaposition of European or American verse with bars of music drawn from the sorrow songs. In contrast to Carroll, however, he regards these pairings less as emblems of African American cultural integrity or the possibility of American racial integration than as marks of rupture and the articulation of difference. According to Theodor Adorno, the synesthetic integration of individual arts in the *Gesamtkunstwerk* was intended to produce "an artifice so perfect that it conceals all the sutures in the final artifact."[23] Whether Du Bois likewise sought to conceal the sutures in his construction of *Souls* is not clear—although Carroll's suggestion that he aspired to reflect and call into being a unified culture may imply as much. In any event, Weheliye's portrait of Du Bois as the "engineer" of a dub mix combining *Souls*'s "phono-epi-graphs" with passages of lyric poetry foregrounds and valorizes *Souls*'s sutures, figuring them not as marking Du Bois's incomplete

21. Here I improvise somewhat on Deleuze's and Guattari's difficult notion of a rhizome. See Gilles Deleuze and Félix Guattari, *A Thousand Plateaus: Capitalism and Schizophrenia*, trans. Brian Massumi (Minneapolis: University of Minnesota Press, 1987), chap. 1, especially 21.

22. Here I gesture ever so briefly to the theme of circulation, which has been productively engaged by previous issues of *Public Culture* and which is very clearly implicated in the issues I raise here relating to *Souls*'s accumulation of political and literary authority. See, for example, Dilip Parameshwar Gaonkar and Elizabeth A. Povinelli, "Technologies of Public Forms: Circulation, Transfiguration, and Recognition," *Public Culture* 15 (2003): 385–97.

23. Theodor Adorno, *In Search of Wagner*, trans. Rodney Livingston (Trowbridge and Esher, U.K.: NLB, 1981), 97.

representation of a "true and authentic African American past" but as future-oriented signs of a new and disruptive Afro-modern temporality.[24]

Drawing on work of Ralph Ellison and Walter Benjamin, Weheliye gives a political inflection to his engagement with Du Bois when he ties *Souls*'s interruption of the temporality of modernity to "the tradition of the oppressed." *Souls*, he claims, is a structural enactment of principles implied in Ellison's meditation on black men's lives "outside the groove of history" and Benjamin's criticism of historicism in the name of a messianic sensibility that would explode the continuum of history—principles that demand a syncopated break with the hegemonic sense of time that Benjamin thought was complicit with the accumulation of the wreckage of history. In Weheliye's reading of *Souls*, the book's collage-like and distinctive "mixology" is an aesthetic formation that projects a time different than the time of oppression.

Weheliye's essay forms an appropriate conclusion to our celebration of *Souls*, for its insistence on the futurity of Du Bois's "fireworks" so effectively challenges the persistent temptation to read it as an expressive artifact of the African American past. *Souls* may indeed have been written in the spirit of an authenticity-based notion of literary and political authority that invites and perhaps justifies romantic accounts of its continuing circulation and authority. But as a dub mix, the book also incarnates a singular, phono-graphic materiality that resists efforts to read it in the spirit of a hermeneutics that would interpret and understand it as a representation of what is genuinely black or African American. To the extent that Du Bois's recordings of the sorrow songs embody such resistance, they may be appreciated in the spirit of Adorno, and with an eye to the recent writing of Fred Moten, as the sources of an antihermeneutical aesthetic negativity that, in Weheliye's words, "disrupt[s] the flow of words" and noisily "implode[s] the linguistic utterances that frame them."[25]

24. Alexander G. Weheliye, "The Grooves of Temporality," in this issue.

25. Weheliye, "The Grooves of Temporality." Here I improvise on Christoph Menke's excellent discussion of the tensions between Gadamerian hermeneutics and Adorno's development of the notion of aesthetic negativity in *The Sovereignty of Art: Aesthetic Negativity in Adorno and Derrida*, trans. Neil Solomon (Cambridge, Mass.: MIT Press, 1998), chap. 1. See also Fred Moten, *In the Break: Aesthetics and the Black Radical Tradition* (Minneapolis: University of Minnesota Press, 2003), especially the introduction and chap. 1.

Robert Gooding-Williams teaches philosophy and African American studies at Northwestern University, where he also is director of the Alice Berline Kaplan Center for the Humanities. He is the author of *Zarathustra's Dionysian Modernism* (2001) and a coeditor of the Bedford Books edition of *The Souls of Black Folk* (1997). His current projects include a book on Du Bois and Douglass as political philosophers and a collection of essays on philosophy, race, politics, and film. Gooding-Williams's coeditor for this special issue, **Dwight A. McBride**, is chair and Leon Forrest Professor of African American Studies at Northwestern University. Author of *Impossible Witnesses: Truth, Abolitionism, and Slave Testimony* (2001) and, most recently, of *Why I Hate Abercrombie and Fitch: Essays on Race and Sexuality* (2005), McBride also edited *James Baldwin Now* (1999) and coedited the 2003 Lambda Literary–winning anthology *Black Like Us: A Century of Lesbian, Gay, and Bi-Sexual African American Fiction* (2002).

Resounding *Souls*:
Du Bois and the African
American Literary Tradition

Cheryl A. Wall

y almost every critical reckoning, *The Souls of Black Folk* ([1903] 1989) is the preeminent statement of modern black consciousness. A fusion of history, sociology, personal memoir, and collective memory, *Souls* is unique in form and unsurpassed in influence among African American texts. Yet it is not on these grounds alone that *Souls* garnered the range of commentators and celebrants for its centenary that it did.[1] In his masterwork, W. E. B. Du Bois drew on African American expressive culture—its music and rhetoric—to produce a singular text that resounds throughout the literary tradition of the twentieth century. Metaphors of the Color Line, the Veil, double consciousness, and the Black Belt inform such African American classics as *The Autobiography of an Ex-Colored Man* (1912), *Cane* (1923), *Invisible Man* (1952), and *Song of Solomon* (1987). In Arnold Rampersad's assessment, "If all of a nation's literature may stem from one book, as Hemingway implied about *The Adventures of Huckleberry Finn*, then it can as accurately be said that all of Afro-American literature of a creative nature has proceeded from Du Bois' . . . *The Souls of Black Folk*."[2]

I thank Donald Gibson, Mae Henderson, and the members of the *Public Culture* editorial committee for their insightful comments and suggestions on earlier versions of this essay.

1. In addition to the conference at Northwestern University, symposia were held at the City University of New York, Morgan State University, the University of Wisconsin–Madison, and the National Black Arts Festival in Atlanta. The city of Newark, New Jersey, selected *Souls* as the text to be read in their "one city/one book" initiative.

2. Arnold Rampersad, *The Art and Imagination of W. E. B. Du Bois* (Cambridge, Mass.: Harvard University Press, 1976), 89.

Public Culture 17(2): 217–34

I concur with that judgment. My argument centers on why and how *Souls* has been foundational to modern African American literature. The most important reason lies in the text's self-consciousness of its participation in an ongoing tradition of African American expressivity. However, as its chapters unfold, *Souls* locates itself in a soundscape that exceeds the limits of textual representation. The distance between what the text can and cannot represent is figured by the musical epigraphs that precede each chapter. The silent bars of music drawn from the Negro spirituals or "sorrow songs," as Du Bois deemed them, are signs for sounds to which the text can at best allude. They represent voices that Du Bois's readers in 1903 could not hear. I read the epigraphs as hieroglyphs that stand in for gaps in the text, gaps that subsequent writers would strive to fill. I end my article with a reading of Toni Morrison's *Song of Solomon*, a novel that creates a fictional terrain evocative of the Black Belt in *Souls*. In her re-sounding of Du Bois, Morrison writes a text as haunting as its precursor.

Although my argument turns on what *Souls* omits, I want first to acknowledge how much it contains. As a multigeneric volume, *Souls* documents the history of the Freedmen's Bureau, the agency established in 1865 that served as the government of the unreconstructed South for seven years. It charts the rise of Booker T. Washington, who is sardonically described as "certainly the most distinguished Southerner since Jefferson Davis," and assesses his role through the historical perspective of black leadership.[3] It compiles statistics on housing and employment. It analyzes the structure of rural black communities, giving data on social class, criminality, and the church. It offers an eloquent brief for the value of liberal arts education and cites the number of black college graduates—400 from white colleges and 2,000 from black institutions—at the time of its writing.

The importance of this data notwithstanding, Du Bois had announced in his preface that the aim of his little book was to "sketch, in vague, uncertain outline, the spiritual world in which ten thousand thousand Americans live and strive" (37). Far from empty-handed supplicants, black folk brought their own estimable gifts—spiritual and aesthetic—to the branch of the kingdom of culture slowly being established in the United States. Consequently, *Souls* testifies to the legacy of the black intellectual and spiritual leader Alexander Crummell. It elegizes those whose potential goes unrealized, including Du Bois's own son, his student Josie, the fictional protagonist John Jones, and his sister Jennie. It presents religious rituals and proclaims the beauty of the sorrow songs, deeming them "the

---

3. W. E. B. Du Bois, *The Souls of Black Folk* (1903; New York: Penguin, 1989), 37. Subsequent references will be made parenthetically to this edition.

singular spiritual heritage of the nation and the greatest gift of the Negro people" (205).

Even the chapters that adhere most closely to the protocols of social science leaven facts with poetry. The chapter on the Freedmen's Bureau, for example, is titled "Of the Dawn of Freedom," and its musical epigraph quotes the majestic theme of the spiritual "My Lord, What a Morning!" The lyrical title captures the promise inherent in the Emancipation moment and the hopes and dreams subsequently invested in the Freedmen's Bureau and its work. The chapter outlines the extent to which the promise was realized—particularly in the schools organized for and by freed slaves—as well as its failures, notably in the reallocation of the abandoned lands that was central to the bureau's charge. The default on the economic promise leaves the slaves freed but hardly free. The spiritual whose opening lines can be heard both as "My Lord, What a Morning" and "My Lord, What a Mourning" measures the distance between the poetry of the promise and the fact of its failure as it weighed on the spirits of black people.[4]

By worrying the line between genres, as it were, *Souls* splinters the opposition between history and memory. As Pierre Nora conceives the terms, history is static while memory is dynamic: "At the heart of history is a critical discourse that is antithetical to spontaneous memory. History is perpetually suspicious of memory, and its true mission is to suppress and destroy it."[5] *Souls* defies this expectation, for Du Bois writes as both a historian and a poet/preserver of the cultural memory encoded in the spirituals. He writes, that is, with the understanding that the "true" history, the then-unwritten history of black Americans, was expressed in their songs and spiritual traditions.[6]

The protagonist of *Souls* is a traveler, unsure of his relationship to the folk who live behind the veil but certain nonetheless that he is connected to them. One of the first texts in the African American tradition to reverse the journey from South

4. In "The Sorrow Songs," Du Bois cites the title as "My Lord, what a mourning!" (208). Eric Sundquist points out the ambiguity of the title and suggests that Du Bois might have chosen the spelling he did "to emphasize its resonance as one of the 'sorrow songs.' " *To Wake the Nations: Race in the Making of American Literature* (Cambridge, Mass.: Harvard University Press, 1993), 1. Charles Nero extends that point in a comment he made in response to this essay. Black English speakers may say/sing "My Lawd, What a Moanin' " and thereby enact the emotion they express.

5. Pierre Nora, "Between Memory and History: *Les lieu de mémoire*," trans. Marc Roudebush, *Representations* 26 (spring 1989): 9.

6. Shamoon Zamir rightly emphasizes the originality of Du Bois's conception of unwritten history. Rather than the inclusion of particular events or specific individuals, Du Bois was "concerned, instead, with uncovering those intricate structures of consciousness that are formed, broken, and re-formed under the slow and daily violence of actual historical process." Zamir, *Dark Voices: W. E. B. Du Bois and American Thought, 1888–1903* (Chicago: University of Chicago Press, 1995), 105.

to North mapped in the slave narratives, *Souls* constitutes what Robert Stepto aptly terms a "cultural immersion ritual."[7] *Souls* documents the *collective* history of Africans in the United States, particularly the difficult and unfinished transition from slavery to freedom, as well as the *personal* history of its author, a northern-born intellectual who is by dint of birth rather than experience "bone of the bone and flesh of the flesh of them that live within the Veil" (2). The text fashions that personal history as a journey. It begins in Great Barrington, Massachusetts, then moves on to Nashville, where Du Bois matriculates at Fisk, and to the rural Tennessee community in which Du Bois the narrator teaches during the summer in a one-room school. It continues from Atlanta to Dougherty County, Georgia, the heart of the Black Belt. At every destination, the narrator encounters a community more unfamiliar to him than the last, more distant from northern customs and mores, and more steeped in the southern expressive traditions honed during slavery. The book ends as Du Bois, in his study at Atlanta University, meditates on the sounds he has heard.

Du Bois's "Black Belt" is the center of the black population in the United States. More than one million African Americans lived in Georgia at the turn of the century; it was the "historic ground" in which the traditions go deepest. The region's rich black soil made it the heart of the antebellum Cotton Kingdom. Du Bois's idea of "historical ground" is very close to Nora's "site of memory," which exists "where memory crystallizes and secretes itself at a particular historical moment, a turning point where consciousness of a break with the past is bound up with the sense that memory has been torn—but torn in such a way as to pose the problem of the embodiment of memory in certain sites where a sense of historical continuity persists."[8]

The historical moment in *Souls* is post-Reconstruction, which, as "Of the Black Belt" illustrates, has proven to be a less decisive break with the past for African Americans than for whites. Blacks' labor was exploited in the Black Belt during slavery; their labor fueled the Confederate war effort when the region became the granary of the Southern troops; and it continued to be exploited after Reconstruction. Continuing, too, is blacks' resistance, sometimes in alliance with Native Americans but more often solitary and unavailing. The present is eerily continuous with the past. The vastness of the landscape, the ruins of the corrupt old social

7. Robert Stepto asserts that "what is extraordinary and absolutely fresh about this ritual is that, in terms of its symbolic geography, it is a journey both to and into the South." Stepto, *From behind the Veil: A Study of Afro-American Narrative*, 2nd ed. (Urbana: University of Illinois Press, 1991), 66.

8. Nora, "Between Memory and History," 7.

order, the harshness of the corrupt new social order, and the isolation of a population in which blacks outnumber whites by five to one render this history in the starkest of terms. These terms are at once documentary and poetic, political and prophetic. Du Bois's phrase "the Egypt of the Confederacy," for example, has the force of biblical allusion, connoting both the bondage of the slaves and the peonage to which the putative freedmen and -women have been delivered. The chapter as a whole is, to quote Eric Sundquist, "the spiritual center" of the book.[9]

Leaving Atlanta, Du Bois's narrator invites his reader to join him in the Jim Crow car, a gesture that reinscribes the narrator's racial difference vis-à-vis the white audience that is announced in the book's preface.[10] But the more telling difference in the later chapter is the experiential gap between the narrator and his racial kin. Detraining in Albany, Georgia, "the centre of the life of ten thousand souls" (95), the narrator remarks on the transformation it undergoes on Saturday as black country folk take "full possession of the town" (94). The narrator does not comment further on this incipient nationalism. Instead, cosmopolitan to his fingertips, he draws flattering comparisons between the black peasants of Albany and their counterparts of the Rhine-Pflaz, Naples, and Cracow—all places where he has himself traveled. Stymied by the July heat, the narrator takes several days to "muster courage enough" to explore the "unknown world" that lies beyond the city limits (95).

This unknown world is marked first by the desolate landscape, with its once fertile soil now exhausted. Little of beauty remains, "only a sort of crude abandon that suggests power,—a naked grandeur as it were" (99). Throughout the chapter Du Bois extends the metaphor of the journey, so that the reader comprehends the scene through the eyes of the uninitiated narrator/observer. Soon the power of the natural landscape is associated with the ruins that symbolize the power of the fallen slave system: "The whole land seems forlorn and forsaken. Here are the remnants of the vast plantations of the Sheldons, the Pellots, and the Rensons; but the souls of them are passed" (96). In their stead are the souls of black folk.

9. Sundquist, *To Wake the Nations*, 503.

10. Du Bois's address to his reader was well earned. As David Levering Lewis notes, the culture and institutions of the rural South "were as mysterious to most early twentieth-century readers as Livingstone's Africa." Lewis makes bold claims for the sociological importance of Du Bois's chapters "Of the Black Belt," "Of the Quest of the Golden Fleece," and "Of the Meaning of Progress": "Not since Frederick Law Olmsted crisscrossed the region before the Civil War, graphically recounting its inefficient productivity, its isolation and ignorance, the sparse luxury even among its seigneurs, and the ubiquity of stunted human and natural material, had there been such a cogent blend of detailed observation and insight." Lewis, *W. E. B. Du Bois—Biography of a Race, 1868–1919* (New York: Holt, 1993), 285.

The transformation from white to black (one day the narrator travels ten miles without seeing a white face) produces odd juxtapositions. Mansions seemingly haunted by the past appear suddenly on the horizon, standing silent amid ashes and tangled weeds. Each scene seems to offer a rebuke to the sins of the past. For example, "the Big House stands in half-ruin, its great front door staring blankly at the street, and the back part grotesquely restored for its black tenant" (97). Another crumbling mansion is "filled now with the grandchildren of the slaves who once waited on its tables" (102). As on those Saturdays when blacks take possession of Albany, these changes are not revolutionary; economic and political power remain in white hands.

Although the narrator expresses sympathy for the heirs of the departed slaveholders ("sad and bitter tales lie hidden back of those white doors"), the text gives voice to the heirs of the slaves, who are left to eke out a living from exhausted land. The narrator stops to interview impoverished sharecroppers, blacksmiths and storekeepers, and a handful of black freeholders. One of the freeholders, a tall bronzed man who "walks too straight to be a tenant," remarks that cotton is down to four cents (97). Another "ragged, brown, and grave-faced man" witnesses slavery: "This land was a little hell. . . . I've seen niggers drop dead in the furrow but they were kicked aside and the plough never stopped" (102). On what was once the Bolton estate, worked for years by black convict labor, the narrator meets laborers who are in fact no more free than their slave ancestors. In response to Du Bois's question of how much rent they pay, one man turns to his neighbor: "I don't know, what is it, Sam?" Sam's answer captures the pervasive despair: "All we make" (105). The laconic voices contest for authority with the erudite and eloquent voice of the narrator.

Du Bois's narrator is quick to cite statistics: 150 barons had ruled 6,000 Negroes; 90,000 acres of tilled land in Dougherty County were valued at $3 million. He is also adept at charting geography and quoting historical references. But he is open to other ways of knowing. One moment in the chapter stands out in this regard. In contrast to the often barren landscape, the narrator comes upon a verdant scene in which "spreading trees spring from a prodigal luxuriance of undergrowth; great dark green shadows fade into the black background, until all is one mass of tangled semi-tropical foliage, marvellous in its weird savage splendor" (100). In this setting, the narrator "could imagine the place under some weird spell, and was half-minded to search out the princess" (99). But rather than a fairy tale, the narrator reenvisions history. In particular he calls to mind Osceola (1800–1838), the leader of the Seminoles, whose heritage was part African American and part Native American. Many fugitive slaves joined his army that he led into battle against the United States during the Seminole War of 1835. Their defeat causes Du Bois's narrator to remark, "small wonder the wood is red" (101). Then in broad impressionistic strokes, he sketches the ensuing history: with no further impediment, the callous planters built what was by 1860 "perhaps the richest slave kingdom the modern world ever knew" (101). The kingdom was characterized by material splendor and moral corruption. The parvenu owners stand in marked contrast to the courageous warrior Osceola.

At the end of the chapter, the narrator seems considerably less estranged from the folk. He sits with a group of people as they tell stories of exploitation and dispossession. Intelligence and industry count for nothing; the talented and the ambitious are cheated as easily as the ignorant. Although the narrator's voice is differentiated by his language and education, for the first time he becomes part of a domestic scene he describes. In the moment he conveys his indignation at the wrong done his fellows, he seems to become aware of the ineffectualness of his hard-won academic knowledge in their world. He explains to one of the group that the sheriff had no right to take his furniture because "furniture is exempt from seizure by law." But the chapter gives the rural black man the last word: "Well, he took it just the same" (110). The world of the Black Belt is one in which neither reason nor law signifies. It is the antithesis of other sites of memory in *Souls*—Fisk and Atlanta universities, for example—where Du Bois is spiritually most at home.

In perhaps the most remarkable gesture in the book, Du Bois uses music, the sorrow songs in particular, to narrow the experiential gap between the collective history of places like Dougherty County and his own. The penultimate chapter begins with his acknowledgment that the sorrow songs had produced a stirring effect on him since childhood, a strange effect that made him know them "as of me and of mine" (204). He emphasizes that he came to this realization in the North, long before he learned anything of the history that produced the songs or, for that matter, of his racial affiliation to those who sang them. He follows this testimony with a description of Jubilee Hall, the landmark building on the Fisk campus that was built with funds raised by the Fisk Jubilee Singers in their performance tours throughout the United States and Europe: "To me Jubilee Hall seemed ever made of the songs themselves, and its bricks were red with the blood and toil. Out of them rose for me morning, noon, and night, bursts of wonderful melody, full of the voices of my brothers and sisters, full of the voices of the past" (204–5).

Jubilee Hall becomes a metonym for the history of Fisk and of African American education more generally. Fisk was founded in Nashville by officers of the

American Missionary Association in 1866 to educate freed slaves. Few students could pay their way, and George L. White, a white American who taught music and served as the school's treasurer, soon organized a student choir to help raise funds. He trained the group to sing anthems, arias, and popular ballads as well as the spirituals most of them already knew; eight of the original nine singers were former slaves. At first the singers performed locally; then in 1871 they embarked on a national tour. Less than two years later they sang a command performance for Queen Victoria. Despite having to resist classification as "minstrels," they enjoyed great success. Critics applauded them, and audiences clamored for their music, especially the spirituals that most whites were hearing for the first time.[11] The choir soon became known as the Fisk Jubilee Singers, a name that commemorated the Emancipation. Within seven years they had taken their music across the United States and Europe and raised $150,000 to support the school.

The Jubilee Singers made spirituals part of the national musical repertoire. The first collection of their songs was published in 1872.[12] Its success led to similar compilations, just as the model of the traveling choir was emulated by black schools and colleges for most of the next century. When Du Bois arrived at Fisk as a student in 1885, he entered a community that preserved and celebrated the slaves' musical legacy. There he heard the "ten master songs," as he deems them (208). In his travels through the Black Belt, he heard the same songs sung not as they were transcribed in books but as they were improvised in churches and tent meetings.

By the time he wrote *Souls*, Du Bois had discerned in the sorrow songs the slave's message to the world, a message that conveys a profound critique of the institution of slavery itself. This critique was the "real poetry and meaning" of the spirituals, the one that lay beneath "conventional theology and unmeaning rhapsody" (210). His interpretation moved the spirituals beyond the domains of religion or entertainment.[13] For Du Bois, the songs not only protest exploitation but

11. Du Bois cites earlier commentators and collectors of spirituals, including Thomas Wentworth Higginson, the white commander of a regiment of African American troops during the Civil War, who wrote about the importance of music in his memoir, *Army Life in a Black Regiment* (1870), and Lucy McKim Garrison, who collected slave songs in the Sea Islands off the coast of South Carolina during the Civil War and helped edit *Slave Songs in the United States* (1867). "But," he concludes, "the world listened only half credulously until the Fisk Jubilee Singers sang the slave songs so deeply into the world's heart that it can never wholly forget them again." Du Bois, *Souls*, 205.

12. See John Lovell, *Black Song: The Forge and the Flame; The Story of How the Afro-American Spiritual Was Hammered Out* (New York: Macmillan, 1972), chap. 25, for a history of the Fisk Jubilee Singers and a discussion of the books published about them.

13. Paul Gilroy notes that "for their liberal patrons the music and song of the Fisk Jubilee Singers offered an opportunity to feel closer to God and to redemption" and a sense of moral rectitude in

inscribe the disruption of family ("mother and child are sung, but seldom father") and emotional exile ("the mountains are well known, but home is unknown") (211). At the same time, the spirituals convey the message of hope, "a faith in the ultimate justice of things" (213). The power of the music is tangible, literally so in the construction of Jubilee Hall. Figuratively, its power continues to preserve the spirits of the dispossessed, even in places like Dougherty County.[14]

But the meditation that closes *Souls* does not end there. From whence came this power? What is the source of the expressive traditions that anchor the soul? For most of the chapter "Of the Sorrow Songs," the focus is on the words of the spirituals, words derived in the main from the Bible. Du Bois, the sociologist, is, of course, concerned with the function of the songs as well. He claims to know nothing about music; he says simply that "the music is far more ancient than the words." To illustrate this point, he transcribes from memory the lyrics and the music of an African song passed down in his family from generation to generation: "We sing it to our children, knowing as little as our fathers what its words may mean, but knowing well the meaning of the music" (207). Scholars have since tried but so far failed to translate the words.[15] The song that begins "*Do bana coba, gene me, gene me!*" is one of only two musical quotations in *Souls* that includes both words and music. Of course, in this instance the words cannot signify. The moment presents a sharp contrast to the bars of music that stand as silent markers at the head of each of the book's chapters.

Scholars have interpreted these epigraphs in various ways. Donald Gibson reads them as "mute ciphers." Contradicting the meaning that he believes Du Bois intended, that blacks and whites are "in essence the same in that they possess souls," Gibson argues that the epigraphs convey instead the chasm between black and white, a chasm "as immense as the social, political, economic and temporal chasm" between the nineteenth-century British poet Arthur Symons and the creators of "Nobody Knows the Trouble I've Seen." In Sundquist's view, the musical

light of their political reformism. Gilroy, *The Black Atlantic: Modernity and Double Consciousness* (Cambridge, Mass.: Harvard University Press, 1993), 90. Well aware as he was of this response and its political usefulness, Du Bois wanted to complicate it by insisting on the political consciousness of the slaves and their descendants as well as the abolitionists and theirs.

14. As Paul Allen Anderson observes, "The songs had outlived legalized slavery as a beacon signaling the ongoing necessity of black liberation." Anderson, *Deep River: Music and Memory in Harlem Renaissance Thought* (Durham, N.C.: Duke University Press, 2001), 30.

15. Sundquist argues that a good measure of the song's significance derives "precisely because it cannot be translated. . . . 'Do bana coba' literalizes the vocalization as an unknown language beyond words, a cry out of the territory of sound that is transgeographical and Pan-African in the most elemental sense." Sundquist, *To Wake the Nations*, 529–30.

epigraphs may be compared to the tradition of African American performance called "lining out." "In this respect," he writes, "the chapters may be seen to improvise upon and extend the ideas laid out in the spiritual epigraphs." At the same time, they constitute "a cultural 'language' that cannot be properly interpreted or even 'heard' at all, since it fails to correspond to the customary mapping of sounds and signs that make up the languages of the dominant (in this case white) culture." Taking into account the difficulties encountered by collectors who sought to transcribe the sounds of the sorrow songs according to the Western system of musical notation, Alexander Weheliye concludes that "the musical notes, like the entire text, form a mix that transforms two distinct parts—Western musical notation and spirituals—into a temporary fusion that calls attention to its own impurity."[16]

In considering *Souls* as a generative text within the African American literary tradition, I suggest that we read the musical epigraph as a hieroglyph. *Hieroglyph* is defined as a figure of some object standing for a word or—in some cases, according to the *Oxford English Dictionary*—a figure standing for a syllable or *sound* and forming an element of a species of writing found on ancient Egyptian monuments and records. An additional definition of the term involves a figure or a device having some hidden meaning. All of these definitions contain associations that are richly suggestive for *Souls*, which invokes, with poetic longing, "the shadow of a mighty Negro past [that] flits through the tale of Ethiopia the Shadowy and of Egypt the Sphinx" (6). More important is the opening reference to the many things that "lie buried" herein, "which if read with patience may show the strange meaning of being black here in the dawning of the Twentieth Century." The musical epigraphs, most but not all of which are identified in the last chapter, contain the most profound meanings that are, as it were, hidden in plain sight.

The epigraphs are of course illegible to those who cannot read musical notation. For those readers, the bars may as well be hieroglyphs. Even readers who can identify the key signatures, the notes, and the number of beats in a measure can only recognize those songs they already know. Far more were acquainted with

16. Donald B. Gibson, "Introduction," in *The Souls of Black Folk*, by W. E. B. Du Bois (New York: Penguin, 1989), xvi; Sundquist, *To Wake the Nations*, 491, 470; and Alexander Weheliye, "In the Mix: Hearing the Souls of Black Folk, *Amerikastudien/American Studies* 45 (2000): 551. Weheliye offers a compelling revisionist interpretation of the relationship between the musical epigraphs taken from the spirituals and the literary epigraphs taken from Western poets. He argues that just as the poems transform the spirituals, the spirituals transform the poems so that Symons's poem, for example, "becomes legible as a lament against the miseries of slavery and a testimony to the 'Spiritual Strivings' of black subjects." Weheliye, "In the Mix," 552.

the melody of "Swing Low, Sweet Chariot" than with "Bright Sparkles in the Churchyard," the spiritual that stands at the beginning of "Of the Black Belt." The latter would be known only by one who had dwelt behind the Veil or had studied long to excavate its meanings. But beyond standing for the sounds that cannot be captured on the page, the epigraphs theorize their meaning.

In the influential essay "The Race for Theory," Barbara Christian argues that rather than the dense abstractions of philosophy, people of color theorize in narrative forms that include stories, riddles, and proverbs. Christian asserts that "my folk . . . have always been a race for theory—though more in the form of the hieroglyph, a written figure that is both sensual and abstract, both beautiful and communicative."[17] Those qualities of the hieroglyph are at work in the epigraphs of *Souls*. They are sensual in that they evoke voiceless sounds; to those whose memories cannot insert those voices, the lines and shapes are abstract figures. They communicate, but they withhold as much as they convey. As hieroglyphs, the bars of music stand for what cannot be written, they figure the gaps in the formidable knowledge Du Bois brings to bear on the history and experience of Africans in America. African American writers who follow Du Bois strive to fill in the gaps—to transcribe that sound and the knowledge it encodes—in their poetry and prose.

The Souls of Black Folk has served as a precursor text for generations of black writers. Perhaps the first to revise it was James Weldon Johnson, who gave fictional form to *Souls* in *The Autobiography of an Ex-Colored Man*. Johnson invents a protagonist who might be considered the anti–Du Bois, a character who consistently draws the wrong messages from his experiences but whose journey is instructive for readers. Jean Toomer infuses *Cane* with the sounds of the spirituals: "Caroling softly souls of slavery/What they were, and what they are to me" (12). Religious shouts grate on the ears of his conflicted protagonist Kabnis, much as they do on the protagonist in *Souls*'s "Of the Coming of John." Like the ex-colored man, the eponymous protagonist of Ellison's classic novel experiences what Du Bois famously formulates as "a peculiar sensation, this double-consciousness, this sense of always looking at one's self through the eyes of others" (5). Ellison works variations on this theme to produce his trope of invisibility, the trope that defines the relation of black people to the white world in his novel. In his essays, moreover, Ellison has been as influential as Du Bois in his appreciation and critique of African American music.[18]

---

17. Barbara Christian, "The Race for Theory," in *African American Literary Theory: A Reader*, ed. Winston Napier (New York: New York University Press, 2000), 281.

18. See, for example, Ralph Ellison, *Shadow and Act* (New York: Random House, 1964).

In Houston Baker's resonant appraisal, *The Souls of Black Folk* is "a singing book."[19] So is *Invisible Man*. So, too, is *Song of Solomon*, as its title announces, a novel that has not to my knowledge been read in dialogue with *Souls*. In fact, the first voice we hear is Pilate's powerful contralto singing:

O Sugarman done fly away
Sugarman done gone
Sugarman cut across the sky
Sugarman gone home.[20]

The last voice we hear is Milkman's, as he sings verses of the same song to the dying Pilate in the novel's final scene. He has deciphered the history the song encoded. *The Souls of Black Folk* and *Song of Solomon* express a shared belief that the unwritten history of black Americans lies buried within their songs. But the connections go deeper: *Song of Solomon* revises and extends *The Souls of Black Folk* in several ways: through a tropological revision of the Black Belt; through the revision of an assertion of racial kinship ("Bone of the bone, flesh of the flesh") to the exploration of family history; and through an extension of the biblical allusions that inform both texts.[21]

To illustrate, I turn to the chapter that relates Milkman's encounter with Circe and introduces the second section of the novel. The chapter begins with an allusion to a fairy tale, Hansel and Gretel, that unlike a similar reference in *Souls* foreshadows the aura of enchantment that will surround the chapter's signal encounter. But, as is true of the novel in general, indirection is the mode of telling. So, before we observe Milkman's meeting with Circe, through whom he will hear vestiges of his ancestor's voice, we watch his preparation for that engagement. While still in Michigan with Guitar, he prepares for a mission he does not pursue. Then in Danville, in his conversations with Reverend Cooper and other friends of his grandfather, Milkman begins to understand what he is searching for. It isn't gold.

19. For Houston Baker's analysis, see *Modernism and the Harlem Renaissance* (Chicago: University of Chicago Press, 1987), 57–69.

20. Toni Morrison, *Song of Solomon* (1977; New York: Plume, 1987), 6. Subsequent references will be made parenthetically to this edition.

21. For a discussion of "tropological revisions" in African American literary tradition, see Henry Louis Gates, *The Signifying Monkey* (New York: Oxford University Press, 1988), xxv. In their introduction to *History and Memory in African American Culture* (New York: Oxford University Press, 1994), Geneviève Fabre and Robert O'Meally point out that a site of memory "may be [a] historical or legendary event or figure, a book or an era, a place or an idea" (7) and include *The Souls of Black Folk* itself among their examples.

By the time he enters the "dark, ruined, evil" house, now overseen by Circe, Milkman has earned the epithet Du Bois chooses for his persona: he is a "weary traveler." He has flown from Michigan to Pittsburgh, taken the bus from Pittsburgh to Danville, and waited four days to get a ride to the abandoned Butler place only to find that it is inaccessible by car. Milkman emerges out of a swamp, "a green maw . . . a greenish-black tunnel, the end of which was nowhere in sight" (238). In the scene where Milkman encounters Circe, Morrison revisits the bare ruins of Du Bois's text. In her novel these ruins are reinhabited by a singular black soul.

Circe, a figure with a "face so old it could not be alive," presides over the ruins of the Butler mansion; she has been servant to the nouveau riche whites who murdered Milkman's grandfather, the first Macon Dead, in order to steal his land (240). Like the masters of the Black Belt, the Butlers have died or scattered, and the house has been left to their one-time retainer. Circe is determined to see the house they lied, stole, and killed for collapse into ruins. Resolved never "to clean it again," she allows the Weimaraners she has inherited from the Butlers to foul the house to their hearts' content. Unlike Du Bois's narrator, Milkman gives in to the landscape's weird spell. He meets Circe in a dream. As much an agent of transformation as her mythical namesake, she provides the information he cannot obtain otherwise. "Sing" is not a command; it is his grandmother's name.

Song of Solomon locates the plantation over which Circe presides outside of Danville, Pennsylvania, far from the historical Black Belt. But the novel's geographical shifts extend, rather than undermine, its relation to *Souls*. At one point Guitar, who tells Milkman that his "whole life is geography," probes the meaning of North and South. The terms depend on each other, but they do not define a difference. As Guitar explains, "But does that mean North is different from South? No way! South is just south of North" (114). All of Morrison's novels redraw the symbolic geography of African American literature and American culture. Just as *The Bluest Eye* (1970) and *Sula* (1974) nationalize African American culture by showing how it was carried by blacks from the South—"They come from Mobile. Aiken. From Newport News. From Marietta. From Meridian"—to Midwestern towns, *Song of Solomon* represents the nationalization of southern white racism in the post-Reconstruction era.[22]

22. This last quote from *The Bluest Eye* links these places with the "sound" of the women's speech. "And the sounds of these places in their mouths make you think of love. When you ask them where they are from, they tilt their heads and say 'Mobile' and you think you've been kissed. They say 'Aiken' and you see a white butterfly glance off a fence with a torn wing. They say 'Nagadoches' and you want to say 'Yes, I will.' You don't know what these towns are like but you love what happens to the air when they open their lips and let their names ease out." Toni Morrison, *The Bluest Eye* (New York: Holt, Rinehart, and Winston, 1970), 63.

Yet if Morrison's novel nationalizes Du Bois's major geographical trope, it particularizes the assertion of kinship. The history that engages Milkman's imagination is the history of his family: "It was a good feeling to come into a strange town and find a stranger who knew your people. All his life he'd heard the tremor in the word: 'I live here, but my *people* . . . ' or: 'She acts like she ain't got no *people*,' or: 'Do any of your *people* live there?' But he hadn't known what it meant: links" (229).[23] Macon Dead resembles the freeholders that Du Bois's narrator admires, but Milkman's fascination with his grandfather's heroic exploits is fueled by the familial connection. He revels in the stories Reverend Cooper and his buddies tell, and he responds in kind with stories about his father's efforts to buy "the Erie Lacka*wan*na" (236). One might be tempted to attribute this shift to the narcissism of Morrison's protagonist, but that would overlook how family history makes female characters more central to *Song of Solomon* than they are to the narrative of Du Bois's solitary quester.[24]

Milkman is, of course, the indulged son and heir of a father who is very much a Bookerite figure, a man whose capacity for love died in the moment he witnessed his father's murder. Macon's materialism and greed are the object of communal censure: "a nigger in business is a terrible thing to see" is Guitar's grandmother's judgment (22). But his cruel and exploitative spirit have equally dire consequences

23. In *Dusk of Dawn: An Essay toward an Autobiography of a Race Concept* (1940; New York: Schocken, 1968), Du Bois amplifies the family history he refers to in *Souls*; he even includes a family tree. In a gesture that resonates with *Song of Solomon*, he concedes, "Absolute legal proof of facts like those here set down is naturally unobtainable. Records of birth are often non-existent, proof of paternity is exceedingly difficult and actual written record rare." He has "relied on oral tradition in my mother's family" as well as the "word and written statement from my paternal grandfather" and what written records are available. These are sufficient, for he concludes, "I have no doubt of the substantial accuracy of the story that I am to tell"(104).

24. Feminist scholars have been critical of the gender politics of *Souls*. Hazel Carby notes the presence of Josie and the myth of Atalanta but observes that neither the young woman nor the city "is a symbol of hope for the future of the African American folk, indeed neither have a viable political, social or intellectual future in Du Bois's text. Although as a student at Fisk he was surrounded by black female intellectuals who were his peers, he was not yet able to imagine a community in which positive intellectual and social transformation could be evoked through female metaphors or tropes." Carby, *Race Men* (Cambridge, Mass.: Harvard University Press, 1998), 20. Historian Joy James acknowledges that "profeminist politics" were a hallmark of Du Bois's career but argues that "a masculinist worldview . . . de-radicalized his gender progressivism." James, "The Profeminist Politics of W. E. B. Du Bois with Respects to Anna Julia Cooper and Ida B. Wells Barnett," in *W. E. B. Du Bois on Race and Culture: Philosophy, Politics, and Poetics*, ed. Bernard W. Bell, Emily Grosholz, and James B. Stewart (New York: Routledge, 1997), 142. *Souls* demonstrates a lack of specificity and consequently an erasure of black women. In its genealogy of race leaders, it offers no mention of Du Bois's black female contemporaries.

at home. He encourages Milkman to exploit his sisters and to treat them as his servants. In an emblematic act, Milkman as a young boy urinates on Lena. As an adult, his attitude toward his sisters—and his mother—is disinterested contempt. Only when he discovers that Corinthians is involved with Porter, a member of the Seven Days, does he show any curiosity about her life. He intervenes to break up her romance, thereby prompting Lena to voice the novel's most explicitly feminist statement (215):

> "You don't know a single thing about either of us . . . but now you know what's best for the very woman who wiped the dribble from your chin because you were too young to know how to spit. Our girlhood was spent like a found nickel on you. . . . Where do you get the *right* to decide our lives?"
>
> "Lena, cool it. I don't want to hear it."
>
> "I'll tell you where. From that hog's gut that hangs down between your legs. Well, let me tell you something, baby brother: you will need more than that."

His sister's words help to propel Milkman on his journey but not because he recognizes their rightness. Like the stories his parents tell him about their past lives, Milkman finds Lena's indictment tiresome. It makes him want to leave. That he can embark on his journey, that he has a quest to undertake, is yet another marker of male privilege; Lena and Corinthians cannot leave the house.[25]

As the novel proceeds, Milkman sheds his sexism, just as he divests himself of his material possessions before meeting Circe. The giving relationship he shares with Sweet, the woman he meets in Shalimar, is one example; his willingness to "surrender" his life in response to Pilate's death is another. Milkman is capable of this ultimate act only because he has learned well the "other ways of knowing" that Pilate has taught. His lessons begin with his first conscious encounter with the aunt his father forbade him to see. He espies her first posed like an ancient mother goddess, "one foot pointed east and one pointed west" (36). The gifts

25. In his analysis of Morrison's revision of classical myth, Michael Awkward notes that Milkman's quest is "inspired by an urge to avoid emotional commitment and familial responsibility." However, in a conclusion that I find complements my reading, Awkward argues that although Milkman seeks familial treasure, "what he finds, after a series of episodes, conforming to traditional monomythic paradigms for the male hero called to adventure, is a mature sense of his familial obligations, an informed knowledge of familial (and tribal) history, and a profound comprehension of tribal wisdom." Awkward, " 'Unruly and Let Loose': Myth, Ideology, and Gender in *Song of Solomon*," in *Negotiating Difference: Race, Gender, and the Politics of Positionality* (Chicago: University of Chicago Press, 1995), 145.

she offers, an apple, lessons in how to boil an egg, and how to make wine, carry symbolic significance. Pilate teaches Milkman how to "be" in the world, from the proper way to greet (and treat) other people to the capacity to gain understanding as well as pleasure from sensual experience. Milkman's acquisition of this knowledge confirms that the other ways of knowing the novel privileges are not women's ways of knowing. It is, rather, the knowledge that enables one to live wholly in this world and perhaps in the next world as well.

In a telling coincidence, one of the epigraphs to "Of the Black Belt" in *Souls* comes from the biblical Song of Solomon (1:5–6):

> I am black but comely, O ye daughter of Jerusalem,
> As the tents of Kedar, as the curtains of Solomon.
> Look not upon me, because I am black
> Because the sun hath looked upon me:
> My mother's children are angry with me;
> They made me the keeper of vineyards;
> But mine own vineyard have I not kept.

Dispossession is the key to the passage, as it is to both *The Souls of Black Folk* and *Song of Solomon*. But Morrison's allusions to the biblical text that inspires her title also serve to deepen the representation of female character. These allusions are richly metaphorical: the sensory images of the biblical text infuse the novel. From the wine, which is a source of ecstasy and wisdom in both the ancient and modern texts, to the gingerroot and other spices that permeate them to the vivid evocations of the pastoral, the novel appropriates the song's imagery. Thematically, however, the representation of human relations is key. "What is extraordinary in the [biblical] *Song*," Alicia Ostriker observes, "is precisely the absence of structural and systemic hierarchy, sovereignty, authority, control, superiority, submission, in the relation of the lovers and in their relation to nature."[26] Pilate is the exemplar of this egalitarian vision in Morrison's novel. She can adhere to it in part because she lives outside of societal structures.

Never married, unaffiliated with any social institution, alienated from her only brother, Pilate has created a home for herself, her daughter, and her granddaughter that moves to its own rhythms. They live in a house without electricity, gas, or running water, "as though progress was a word that meant walking a little farther on down the road" (27). Pilate, a woman who makes wine for a living, is as unimpressed with status as with technology. Although she is not naive about social

26. Alicia Ostriker, "A Holy of Holies: The Song of Songs as Counter-Text" (lecture, Rutgers University, New Brunswick, N.J., February 18, 1997).

realities (she knows, for example, how to play the "stage Negro" when doing so is necessary to keep Milkman out of jail), she accepts people with equanimity. Macon's money and position, which mean everything to him, mean nothing to her. Music and memory pervade her home.

At the end of *Song of Solomon*, Milkman *is* able to decode most of the lyrics of the song whose music he has been hearing since the day he was born. He is able to identify the African ancestor and to recognize himself as a son of Solomon. Moreover, when he revises the song to address "Sugar*girl*," he inserts Pilate into the family line (336). Yet Milkman's quest has succeeded in part at the cost of his sister (and cousin) Hagar's life. The dark but comely daughter of Solomon, whose beauty Milkman fails to recognize, is sacrificed. Little wonder then that despite the honor the novel accords the family's history of resistance and struggle, and despite Milkman's belated recognition of his complicity in Hagar's death, this family is always already "Dead."

Many points of difference exist between Du Bois's text and Morrison's, but surely a major one is in how they *sound*. In contrast to the silent bars of music in *Souls*, that only the musically literate and culturally knowledgeable can hear, Morrison invents language that resounds in the reader's consciousness. The mono-syllables of the farmers in the Black Belt give way to the polyphonic vernacular voices of the Blood Bank and Shalimar. Rather than competing with the narrator's voice, these voices extend, clarify, and revise one another's stories. With their blues inflections and the profusion of metaphor that Zora Neale Hurston described as the "will to adorn,"[27] these voices enact the sounds and the meanings necessarily hidden in Du Bois's hieroglyph. In 1903 readers could not have heard these voices.

Although no spaces comparable to the barbershop or the store exist for the female characters in *Song of Solomon*, they tell some of the most memorable stories. Typically they tell these stories, rich in biblical allusion, in private conversations; often they recount family histories. But collective meanings inhere in these personal histories. These stories, like Du Bois's narratives, reveal the souls of black folk. A story that Pilate tells about a time before her brother was destroyed by his materialism and greed may be read as a gloss on the novel's representation of a heterogeneous black community (40–41):

> Hadn't been for your daddy, I wouldn't be here today. I would have died in the womb. And died again in the woods. Those woods and the dark would

27. Zora Neale Hurston, "Characteristics of Negro Expression" (1934; reprinted in *Zora Neale Hurston: Folklore, Memoirs, and Other Writings*, ed. Cheryl A. Wall [New York: Library of America 1995]), 831–34.

have surely killed me. . . . We were lost then. And talking about dark! You think dark is just one color, but it ain't. There're five or six kinds of black. Some silky, some woolly. Some just empty. Some like fingers. And it don't stay still. It moves and changes from one kind of black to another. Saying something is pitch black is like saying something is green. What kind of green? Green like my bottles? Green like a grasshopper? Green like a cucumber, lettuce, or green like the sky is just before it breaks loose to storm? Well, night black is the same way. May as well be a rainbow.

A blues singer as well as a storyteller, Pilate limns a poetic image of blackness that is filled with metaphor and simile. Blackness to Pilate is not a Veil, but a rainbow. She speaks as one for whom the Veil no longer exists, as one determined to construct her own reality and to live fully within it. Pilate is the novel's consummate artist. At the end of *Song of Solomon*, Milkman learns to hear her voice just as Du Bois's narrator in *Souls* has learned to hear the voices of black folk.

In his grand pronouncement at the beginning of the "Sorrow Songs," Du Bois states, "And so by fateful chance the Negro folk-song—the rhythmic cry of the slave—stands to-day not simply as the sole American music, but as the most beautiful expression of human experience borne this side the seas" (205). As rich in philosophical, historical, sociological, and political understandings as *Souls* is, none of its insights is more important than this. Bereft of political rights, economic power, or access to education, black people in slavery and in freedom honed their gifts of the imagination and the spirit. Du Bois stands both inside and outside the scenes he narrates. He is at once historian, poet, and prophet. As a historian he brings academic modes of inquiry to bear on his subject. But as a poet and prophet, he takes his charge from the "black and unknown bards"[28] who created the sorrow songs. He plumbs the depths of African Americans' experience, sounding its beauty and unmasking its horrors. His art, like that of the spirituals, derives from a tragic sensibility, one that is grounded in history but not bound by it. *Souls* enters, interprets, and extends an ongoing tradition; its echoes and its silences continue to resound.

Cheryl A. Wall teaches African American literature in the English department at Rutgers University in New Brunswick, New Jersey. Her latest book is *Worrying the Line: Black Women Writers, Lineage, and Literary Tradition* (2005).

---

28. I take the phrase from the poem "O Black and Unknown Bards" by James Weldon Johnson, anthologized in his *The Book of American Negro Poetry* (1921; New York: Harcourt Brace, 1969), 123–24.

Du Bois and Art Theory: *The Souls of Black Folk* as a "Total Work of Art"

Anne E. Carroll

One of the most striking aspects of W. E. B. Du Bois's *The Souls of Black Folk* (1903) is the author's use of lines of poetry and bars of song to open each of the book's fourteen chapters. Each inscription includes a few lines or stanzas of poetry by writers from America and Europe, such as James Lowell, Lord Byron, or Friedrich von Schiller, paired with one or two bars of song. How the reader should understand these epigraphs is not immediately clear, though, for they include just the lines, the notes, and the poets' names, without explanations or even titles. Indeed, throughout the first thirteen chapters of the book, Du Bois was silent about these epigraphs; they remain cultural inscriptions that we, as readers, must decipher. Only in his last chapter did Du Bois refer to them, and his commentary here is focused more broadly on what he called "the sorrow songs," the spirituals sung by slaves and their descendants, than on the epigraphs themselves. Here Du Bois indicated that the bars of song are symbols of the rich cultural achievements of African Americans; readers come to understand that they are part of his assertion of the importance of African Americans in America's cultural, spiritual, and material development. But even in this final chapter, Du Bois said little about the pairing of songs and poems. What, then, are we to make of these combinations?

We can understand the epigraphs simply as unifying elements of the book or as a signal of Du Bois's argument about the songs' artistic value. But if we consider *Souls* in the context of theories about relations among the arts in the mid-to-late

Public Culture 17(2): 235–54

nineteenth century, its combinations of music and poetry illuminate an as yet unappreciated aspect of Du Bois's creation. In particular, reading Du Bois's book in light of ideas about the "total work of art," especially as advocated by opera composer and theorist Richard Wagner, draws our attention to Du Bois's successful appropriation of theories about the unity of the arts to his goal of undermining American racism.[1] Indeed, *Souls* can be read as a total work of art in the sense advocated by Wagner. But *Souls* is a different kind of artwork than Wagner's operas, both in form and in politics. Du Bois extended the concepts outlined by Wagner, using them to create a new and distinctive kind of text suited to the struggle against racism in the United States. Evaluating his book as a total work of art, then, enhances our appreciation of its innovative form and of Du Bois's creative and intellectual achievement.

Admittedly, the extent to which Du Bois intentionally applied ideas like Wagner's to the composition of *Souls* is unclear. There is little evidence in his published writing to link the book to these concepts about the arts.[2] But there is significant cultural and textual evidence that suggests the relevance of the idea of the total work of art to *Souls*. It seems highly unlikely, moreover, that Du Bois would have been unfamiliar with the concept. For one thing, Wagner and his theories about the unity of the arts were widely disseminated and hugely influential in Germany in the years when Du Bois lived there as a graduate student. Wagner, who began to compose operas and publish essays about the arts during the 1840s, was one of many Romantic artists who were frustrated with what they saw as an unfortunate

1. Du Bois scholars have identified numerous ways in which Du Bois applied the ideas of German intellectuals to the situations of African Americans, but as Russell A. Berman points out, "the nexus of Du Bois and Wagner has not been scrutinized." Berman, "Du Bois and Wagner: Race, Nation, and Culture between the United States and Germany," *German Quarterly* 70 (1997): 127 and 134n32. Berman offers a brief overview of other scholars' assessments of Du Bois's use of German philosophy. "Du Bois and Wagner," 126–27.

2. Oddly, Du Bois devotes little attention to *Souls* in his autobiographies. He mentions it briefly in *Dusk of Dawn: An Essay toward an Autobiography of a Race Concept* (1940; New Brunswick, N.J.: Transaction, 2002) but not at all in *The Autobiography of W. E. B. Du Bois: A Soliloquy on Viewing My Life from the Last Decade of Its First Century* (New York: International, 1968). *Souls* does not even appear in the "calendar" of Du Bois's public life that appears near the end of the latter book. Du Bois published a short essay on *Souls* in the *Independent* in 1904, but it includes no discussion of any influences on the composition of the book. See Du Bois, "The Souls of Black Folk," reprinted in *The Souls of Black Folk*, ed. David W. Blight and Robert Gooding-Williams (Boston: Bedford, 1997), 254–55. If Du Bois explicitly linked Wagner to *Souls* in his unpublished papers, David Levering Lewis does not mention this in his biography of Du Bois, for which he drew heavily on those papers. See Lewis, *W. E. B. Du Bois—Biography of a Race, 1868–1919* (New York: Holt, 1993). I have been unable to find any explicit references to *Souls* as a total work of art in published letters to or from Du Bois or in reviews from the period.

fragmentation of the arts. They believed that, in isolated form, works of art failed to have a sufficient effect on their readers or viewers. They hoped that creating works that involved multiple media, and thus reuniting the arts, might allow them to create texts that had a stronger impact. This goal was particularly widespread among English and German theorists and artists in the late eighteenth and early nineteenth centuries.[3] Those who attempted to create unified arts combined music and literature, music and the visual arts, and even music and odors or colors.[4] They hoped, by doing so, to give their work synaesthesic properties, to create texts that appealed to more than one of the senses of the audience members.[5] The stage often was the locus of these efforts, as the performance arts offered numerous possibilities for combining different kinds of stimuli.

Wagner's explorations of these ideas were particularly influential. In fact, the German term for a total work of art, *Gesamtkunstwerk*, still is largely associated with Wagner.[6] His theoretical musings on the concept, particularly the long essays "The Art-Work of the Future" (1850) and "Opera and Drama" (1851), are seminal statements of its dimensions and possibilities.[7] In them, he criticized opera as it

3. For overviews of these developments, see Günter Berghaus, "A Theater of Image, Sound, and Motion: On Synaesthesia and the Idea of a Total Work of Art," *Maske und Kothurn* 32, nos. 1–2 (1986): 11–14; Thomas Jensen Hines, *Collaborative Form: Studies in the Relations of the Arts* (Kent, Ohio: Kent State University Press, 1991), 1; and Jack M. Stein, *Richard Wagner and the Synthesis of the Arts* (Detroit, Mich.: Wayne State University Press, 1960), 3–5. Berghaus also points out that efforts to combine various media in the theater happened as early as the sixteenth and seventeenth centuries, but he emphasizes that it was the Romantics who first "produced a body of theoretical literature on how this Utopian idea might be achieved." Berghaus, "A Theater," 11–12. Berghaus, Hines, and Stein list an extensive number of participants in these experiments; some of the most recognizable names include Friedrich W. J. Schelling, who was a particularly influential philosopher and advocate of such practices; the writer and artist William Blake; the composers Robert Schumann, Franz Peter Schubert, Hugo Wolf, and Claude Debussy; the writers and theorists Gotthold Lessing, Johann von Herder, Johann von Goethe, Friedrich von Schiller, and Philipp Otto Runge; and the painters Joseph Turner, James Whistler, and Eugene Delacroix.

4. Berghaus discusses efforts to create "colour clavichords" and "clavichords of odours" as well as "theatrical spectacles" that combined sound, colors, and smells. Berghaus, "A Theater," 7–11. Wolfgang Domling focuses on attempts at the "musicalization of painting"; see "Reuniting the Arts: Notes on the History of an Idea," *19th Century Music* 18, no. 1 (1994): 3–9.

5. Berghaus, "A Theater," 10, 16.

6. The link between Wagner and the ideal of the *Gesamtkunstwerk* is so often assumed that recent scholars have been careful to draw attention to the other theorists and practitioners who contributed to the development of the concept. Hines, for example, emphasizes that "the idea had been the public dream of the earlier generations of Romantic poets and composers." Hines, *Collaborative Form*, 3. Berghaus, Stein, and Domling make similar arguments. All four, however, assert Wagner's crucial role in disseminating and popularizing this idea.

7. English translations of these and other essays are available in William Ashton Ellis, trans., *Richard Wagner's Prose Works*, 8 vols. (1892; St. Clair Shores, Mich.: Scholarly Press, 1972). The

had developed through the early to mid-1800s. For example, he believed that too many operas were created as "a succession of vocal numbers, . . . an almost random assemblage of elements that were only remotely related to one another and, quite simply, did not cohere"; he also believed that the proper relation between the poetry and music had yet to be achieved.[8] He also used the essays to posit Greek drama as a model of creative work in which words, music, and gestures were united, and he outlined his ideas about how opera could become a similarly totalizing and synthesizing art form. His was not merely an aesthetic goal, for he believed that if the various elements in opera—music, poetry, song, and the visual appeal of sets, costumes, and the movement of the actors—were brought together into an integrated whole, the resulting accumulation of effects would give the total work more capacity to affect German culture, to unify its people, and to promote a national spirit.[9] But Wagner also believed that the kind of fusion and spirit opera could inspire in its audience was only likely to occur in an ideal setting in which every aspect of a performance could be carefully controlled. With that in mind, he launched a series of national festivals that centered around performances of his operas and that were held at a specially constructed theater in the city of Bayreuth starting in 1876.[10]

There is some debate among Wagner scholars about whether his operas, including those performed at Bayreuth, ever fully realized the ideal of a *Gesamtkunstwerk* or, conversely, whether one form of art, usually music, remained dominant.[11] Importantly, Wagner's ideas about the proper relationship between music, poetry, and drama changed over time. In his earlier statements, he argued that all should have equal roles and that their unity should evolve from "an interdependence of equals"; later, he asserted that music was the most important of the arts.[12] But he always maintained that words and music "could be combined to produce concen-

---

nearly 400–page "Opera and Drama" constitutes the entirety of volume 2. Frank W. Glass summarizes its main points in *The Fertilizing Seed: Wagner's Concept of the Poetic Intent* (Ann Arbor, Mich.: UMI Research Press, 1983), 17–59.

8. Glass, *The Fertilizing Seed*, 23–24.

9. Glass, *The Fertilizing Seed*, 21.

10. Stewart Spencer, "Bayreuth and the Idea of a Festival Theatre," in *The Wagner Compendium: A Guide to Wagner's Life and Music*, ed. Barry Millington (New York: Schirmer/Macmillan, 1992), 167–70; David C. Large, "The Bayreuth Legacy," in Millington, *The Wagner Compendium*, 389–92.

11. Glass offers an overview of this debate in *The Fertilizing Seed*, 5–15.

12. Hines, *Collaborative Form*, 2. Stein also describes this shift in Wagner's thinking, particularly as it was influenced by Wagner's reading of Arthur Schopenhauer's theories of the relations among the arts. Stein, *Richard Wagner*, 6–7.

trated, emotionally satisfying" art.[13] It is that insistence on the potential effects of combining music and art that is so relevant to *Souls*.

It is clear that Du Bois was familiar with Wagner's operas and with relevant aspects of German philosophy long before he published *Souls*. Du Bois had been intrigued with German nationalism since at least 1888, when he graduated from Fisk University and delivered a commencement address on Otto von Bismarck that praised the German chancellor's ability to make "a nation out of a mass of bickering peoples."[14] At Harvard University, where Du Bois earned his Bachelor of Arts in 1890, his concentration was in philosophy, and his studies included classes that covered German philosophy.[15] In the midst of his graduate work at Harvard, he received a fellowship that allowed him from 1892 to 1894 to study at the University of Berlin, where he took courses in economics, history, and sociology.[16] Du Bois also immersed himself in the arts. Decades later, describing his years in Germany, he wrote that he "came to know Beethoven's symphonies and Wagner's *Ring*," a series of four operas that is one of the composer's best-known works. In the same paragraph, Du Bois also mentioned other kinds of works of art: "I looked long at the colors of Rembrandt and Titian. I saw in arch and stone and steeple the history and striving of men and also their taste and expression. Form, color and words took new combinations and meanings."[17] This passage indicates Du Bois's early exposure to Wagner, but it also sets it in the context of his interest in other classical music, the visual arts, and architecture. It is clear, then, that Du Bois developed his familiarity with German cultural and nationalist theory while he was in Germany but, also, that he nurtured his appreciation for many forms of art while there.[18]

When Du Bois returned to the United States in 1894, he reentered America at a time when Wagner and his theories were receiving a fair amount of attention here. Opera was very popular and reached large audiences in the nineteenth century in America; by the turn of the century, though, opera began to be seen as "a 'higher'

13. Glass, *The Fertilizing Seed*, 22.

14. Du Bois, *Autobiography*, 126. Du Bois, of course, believed a similar unification was needed among African Americans.

15. Lewis, *W. E. B. Du Bois*, 100.

16. Lewis offers the most thorough discussion of these years in Du Bois's life; see *W. E. B. Du Bois*, 79–149.

17. Du Bois, *Autobiography*, 156.

18. Du Bois's interest in the visual arts is also evident in his essay on "The Art and Art Galleries of Modern Europe" and in the fact that, while he was in Paris on his way from Germany back to the United States, he " 'haunted' the Louvre where he made elaborate notes on the collections." Lewis, *W. E. B. Du Bois*, 138, 147.

form of art demanding a cultivated audience."[19] Appreciation for Wagner's operas grew with that shift. Wagner festivals had been held in New York and Boston in the 1870s, and his operas were performed across the country in the following decades. By the 1890s, "the cult of Wagner dominated America's musical high culture."[20] In fact, the mid-1890s were the peak years of summer opera festivals, including those at Brighton Beach on Coney Island, where Wagner's music was by far the greatest draw.[21] Furthermore, Wagner's writings had been "widely read in intellectual circles" for decades.[22] Du Bois's work in these years included teaching at Wilberforce University, the University of Pennsylvania, and Atlanta University but also composing the speeches and essays that would become the foundation of *Souls*.

In short, Du Bois's intellectual development and his early exploration of ideas that he would articulate in *Souls* happened at a time and in two countries in which Wagner and his ideas were part of the cultural zeitgeist. Du Bois's awareness of Wagner's work, furthermore, is explicitly signaled by references to one of the composer's operas in *Souls*. In "Of the Coming of John," the one short story in the book, the main character attends a performance of Wagner's *Lohengrin*. This character, a black man named John Jones, is seated next to and snubbed by his white double, John Henderson. The two Johns had grown up together, but here the color line divides them. John Henderson objects to being seated next to a black man, and John Jones is forced to leave the opera house. Later, Jones finds the other attacking his sister; he kills Henderson, and as he waits for an angry mob to find and murder him, he hums the wedding march from the opera.[23]

19. Lawrence W. Levine, *Highbrow/Lowbrow: The Emergence of Cultural Hierarchy in America* (Cambridge, Mass.: Harvard University Press, 1988), 102; for Levine's overview of the popularity of opera in nineteenth-century America, see 85–100. He points out that Wagner was one of the proponents of a distinction between "serious" and "frivolous" opera, which fed into changing attitudes toward opera around the turn of the century. Levine, *Highbrow/Lowbrow*, 100–102.

20. Joseph Horowitz, *Wagner Nights: An American History* (Berkeley: University of California Press, 1994), 2. Horowitz offers an extensive exploration of Wagner's popularity in the United States, including synopses and information about the American premieres of Wagner's operas. Horowitz, *Wagner Nights*, 345–52.

21. Horowitz, *Wagner Nights*, 199–212. Horowitz points out that these festivals were referred to by some as an "American Bayreuth" (17).

22. Horowitz, *Wagner Nights*, 30.

23. The reference to this song in particular probably would have resonated with Du Bois's readers, as the song was one of those well known in American popular music. Levine, *Highbrow/Lowbrow*, 96. Eric J. Sundquist identifies Du Bois's use of the song in *To Wake the Nations: Race in the Making of American Literature* (Cambridge, Mass.: Harvard University Press, 1993), 522. Berman argues that the entire chapter about John can be read as a rewriting of Wagner's opera. Berman, "Du Bois and Wagner," 127–31.

Du Bois's use of Wagner's opera makes sense in many ways. First, the opera touches on themes of love, loyalty, and identity that were of interest to Du Bois, in *Souls* and elsewhere. In the opera, the knight Lohengrin comes to the aid of Elsa, who has been falsely accused of murdering her brother. Lohengrin clears her name, and they wed, but when she is unable to keep her promise to never ask his name or where he is from, he must leave her. John Jones, similarly, who has returned to his hometown from college, defends his sister but must then leave her, for reasons connected to his identity.[24] Wagner's opera also is a fitting allusion for *Souls* because Du Bois experienced his time in Germany as a pleasant—though not unmarred—escape from American racism, and citing the opera may have been a way for him to evoke his enjoyable engagement with Europeans and European culture.[25] Fittingly, Du Bois described Wagner's music as offering escape: when John hears it, it stirs in him a longing "to rise with that clear music out of the dirt and dust of that low life that held him prisoned and befouled."[26] The opera also awakens John's sense of his own power. Although the possibility of transcendence and empowerment is tragically cut short for John, they fit the optimism of *Souls* as a whole. Finally, like Du Bois, Wagner was "engaged in the creation of national heroic art" and saw "culture and, especially, music as the vehicle for a national rejuvenation."[27] In other words, Wagner was interested in creating an art form that reflected and called into being a unified German culture, just as Du Bois was concerned to do for African American culture—and, indeed, for American culture.

But the reference to *Lohengrin* also makes sense because the opera seems to have been, to Du Bois, a particularly clear example of the potential of a work of art that unified different media. When Du Bois described the opera in a newspaper column years later, he emphasized its successful fusion of elements. He

24. For a summary of *Lohengrin*, see Barry Millington, "The Music: Operas: *Lohengrin*," in Millington, *The Wagner Compendium*, 283. Stanley Brodwin, who offers a brief comparison of the opera and Du Bois's story, argues that the contrasts between Lohengrin's status as an esteemed knight and John's violent end "symbolize two contradictory states of being" that illuminate the realities of racism in America. See Brodwin, "The Veil Transcended: Form and Meaning in W. E. B. Du Bois' 'The Souls of Black Folk,'" *Journal of Black Studies* 2, no. 3 (1972): 317–18.

25. Du Bois's sense of the contrast between America's omnipresent and oppressive racism and Europe's relative freedom are hinted at in his comment about coming back to the United States in 1894: in Europe, he wrote, "I dreamed and loved and wandered and sang; then after two long years I dropped suddenly back into 'nigger'-hating America!" Du Bois, *Autobiography*, 183.

26. Du Bois, *Souls*, 177.

27. Sundquist, *To Wake the Nations*, 577; Berman, "Du Bois and Wagner," 131. Neither mentions Wagner's ideas about the possibilities of a total work of art in their discussions of Du Bois's citations of the composer's work.

called *Lohengrin* "one of the few operas which I know by long acquaintance"; his knowledge of it, he claimed, meant he had insight into "some of the secrets and aims of its creator." He cited Wagner's themes and then listed his techniques: "He uses myth, he uses poetry, he uses sound and sight, music and color. And he uses human actors on a stage. The result is beautiful, as in the bride-song, but it is more than that: it rises to a great and glorious drama, which at times reaches the sublime."[28] Du Bois's movement here from the opera's elements to its impact suggests that he felt that the combination of the arts in the opera was integral to its effect; perhaps he had this in mind when he combined music and poetry in *Souls*.

The allusions to *Lohengrin* in *Souls* also draw attention to the ways that Wagner's strategies for enhancing the effectiveness of an opera are echoed in Du Bois's book. Du Bois had clear social and political goals for *Souls*, which are laid out in his "Forethought": he asserted that he wanted to raise the Veil that separated black and white Americans, allowing the "Gentle Reader" who did not understand "the strange meaning of being black" to see into African Americans' experiences, to come to understand their material and spiritual lives.[29] To do so—to educate his readers, in other words—Du Bois presented them with facts and information. Du Bois's training as a sociologist and a historian is relevant here: *Souls* includes both meticulous accounts of historical events of the previous decades and descriptions and analyses of the experiences and attitudes of African Americans.[30] But presenting information was never his end goal: ideally, this shared knowledge would change his readers' understandings of African Americans. *Souls* clearly was a tool Du Bois used to work toward his lifelong ambitions of undermining racism, increasing the opportunities of African Americans, and ensuring their protection from racism and violence. But whether the book could meet those goals, and how it could be as persuasive as possible, were questions of grave concern to Du Bois.

Du Bois's first challenge was to make his book into a coherent whole. He had published a number of its component essays in literary magazines by the turn of the century, and when the publishing firm of A. C. McClurg asked him to collect

28. Du Bois, "Forum of Fact and Opinion: 'Lohengrin,'" *Pittsburgh Courier*, October 31, 1936; reprinted in *Newspaper Columns by W. E. B. Du Bois*, comp. and ed. Herbert Aptheker (White Plains, N.Y.: Kraus-Thomson, 1986), 130.

29. Du Bois, *Souls*, 34.

30. In its sociological aspects, *Souls* has similarities to Du Bois's work at Atlanta University, particularly the annual monographs published under his direction from 1896 to 1914. See Dan S. Green and Edwin D. Driver, eds., *W. E. B. Du Bois on Sociology and the Black Community* (Chicago: University of Chicago Press, 1978), 11–17.

the pieces into a book, he was not at first particularly enthusiastic. As he remembered years later, he had worried that "books of essays almost always fall so flat."[31] When he agreed to publish his essays in one volume, he revised the essays significantly, added some new ones, and otherwise worked to transform this "collection of texts" into an "integrated narrative."[32] Wagner's innovations in opera perhaps offered Du Bois a model: in contrast to the operas that lacked unity, that were collections of individual songs rather than coherent wholes, Wagner used more continuous flow between the songs in his works, and he also developed the practice of infusing each opera with a series of leitmotifs, repeating melodies that changed and developed through the entire work.[33] He believed that, through such repetition, ideas "would accumulate additional layers of significance through their modified reappearance" and the whole text would achieve "a compelling sense of larger structural unity."[34] When the various arts were used to present the leitmotif, the effect was enhanced: Wagner believed that "by expressing an artistic idea simultaneously in different media," the artist could create "a monumental style" that had an "accumulation of effects."[35] In *Souls*, the bars of song and lines of poetry function as these kinds of elements; they visually and symbolically tie together the fourteen chapters of the book, making it more than just the sum of its parts. In other words, they become a graphic leitmotif. But they also contain thematic leitmotifs: ideas present in one element of Du Bois's text are repeated and developed in others, just as they are in Wagner's operas.[36]

Du Bois's use of poems and spirituals that give voice to the same ideas turn the epigraphs and essays into echoing refrains. There are parallels, for example, between the themes of the songs and the messages of Du Bois's own writing:

31. Du Bois, *Dusk of Dawn*, 80.

32. Robert B. Stepto, *From behind the Veil: A Study of Afro-American Narrative*, 2nd ed. (Urbana: University of Illinois Press, 1991), 53; for descriptions of Du Bois's editing process, see 52–91.

33. Thomas S. Grey, "The Music Drama and Its Antecedents: Reminiscence Motif and Leitmotif," in Millington, *The Wagner Compendium*, 79–82. Grey also points out that, though the term *leitmotif* did not originate with the composer himself, it has become the "most famous of all Wagnerian terms." See Grey, "A Wagnerian Glossary: 'Leitmotif,'" in Millington, *The Wagner Compendium*, 234.

34. Grey, "A Wagnerian Glossary: 'Leitmotif,'" 235.

35. Berghaus, "A Theater," 16.

36. Even so, Du Bois apparently was unconvinced that *Souls* worked as a unified whole. In his 1904 essay about the book, Du Bois wrote that it still had "considerable, perhaps too great, diversity," that its "rather abrupt transitions of style, tone and viewpoint" might make it seem disjointed. However, he insisted that it had a unity of purpose and tone and a clear central message. See Du Bois, "The Souls of Black Folk," 254–55.

he wrote in his final chapter of the "strange blending of love and helplessness" in the lyrics of one song and of the cry of the parent who bids farewell to "my only child," ideas that are repeated in Du Bois's own sorrow as expressed in his chapter on the death of his son.[37] There also are parallels between the message of the songs and the poems he used as epigraphs earlier in the book. A line from the spiritual "Nobody Knows the Trouble I've Seen" opens the first chapter, and it is paired with a poem by Arthur Symons in which the speaker offers a plaintive lament for his or her troubles and longing for rest (see fig. 1). The speaker voices despair that there shall be none, worrying that the crying will be "without avail."[38] These emotions are quite fitting for the song, which Du Bois described in the final chapter as the one an old woman sang when the news came that the U.S. government was refusing to grant land to freed slaves.[39] These lines and the song also suit the chapter as a whole, in which Du Bois offered an overview of the hopefulness about freedom and Emancipation—and then the deep disappointment felt by African Americans when the failure of Reconstruction became clear.

Similarly, the lines of poetry and music that open the second chapter relate to one another and to the content of the chapter. The verse is a stanza from a poem by James Russell Lowell called "The Present Crisis," a long call to arms that insists on the need for its readers to battle slavery (see fig. 2).[40] The crisis in Du Bois's chapter is not the Civil War but the post-Reconstruction era; this is the chapter where Du Bois narrated the efforts of the Freedman's Bureau, bemoaning the fact that former slaves were "intimidated, beaten, raped, and butchered by angry and revengeful men."[41] The song is "My Lord, what a mourning!" which Du Bois called in his final chapter "the song of the End and the Beginning," a description that hints at the relentlessness of the crises discussed in the poem and this second essay.[42] Similar thematic links can be made in each of the chapters: each song relates to the lines of poetry with which it is paired and to the chapter the two introduce. In short, music, poetry, and essays present repeating ideas. If Wagner was right about leitmotifs—that they unify a text and enhance its message—the repetitions in *Souls* heighten its effect.

37. Du Bois, *Souls*, 190.
38. Du Bois, *Souls*, 37.
39. Du Bois, *Souls*, 188.
40. The poem, incidentally, would serve a few years later as the source of the name of *The Crisis* magazine, the monthly publication of the NAACP, which Du Bois launched in 1910. See Lewis, *W. E. B. Du Bois*, 409.
41. Du Bois, *Souls*, 57.
42. Du Bois, *Souls*, 188.

I

Of Our Spiritual Strivings

O water, voice of my heart, crying in the sand,
  All night long crying with a mournful cry,
As I lie and listen, and cannot understand
    The voice of my heart in my side or the voice of the sea,
O water, crying for rest, is it I, is it I?
    All night long the water is crying to me.

Unresting water, there shall never be rest
  Till the last moon droop and the last tide fail,
And the fire of the end begin to burn in the west;
    And the heart shall be weary and wonder and cry like the sea,
All life long crying without avail,
    As the water all night long is crying to me.

ARTHUR SYMONS.

Between me and the other world there is ever an unasked question: unasked by some through feelings of delicacy; by others through the difficulty of rightly framing it. All, nevertheless, flutter round it. They approach me in a half-hesitant sort of way, eye me curiously or compassionately, and then, instead of saying directly, How does it feel to be a problem? they say, I know an excellent colored man in my town; or, I fought at Mechanicsville;[2] or, Do not these Southern outrages make your blood boil? At these I smile, or am interested, or reduce the boiling to a simmer, as the occasion may require. To the real question, How does it feel to be a problem? I answer seldom a word.

And yet, being a problem is a strange experience,—peculiar even for one who has never been anything else, save perhaps in babyhood and in Europe. It is in the early days of rollicking boyhood that the rev-

Figure I *From* The Souls of Black Folk *(Bedford, 1997: 37), used with permission*

II

Of the Dawn of Freedom

Careless seems the great Avenger;
  History's lessons but record
One death-grapple in the darkness
  'Twixt old systems and the Word;
Truth forever on the scaffold,
  Wrong forever on the throne;
Yet that scaffold sways the future,
  And behind the dim unknown
Standeth God within the shadow
  Keeping watch above His own.
                   LOWELL.

The problem of the twentieth century is the problem of the color-line,
—the relation of the darker to the lighter races of men in Asia and Africa,
in America and the islands of the sea. It was a phase of this problem that
caused the Civil War; and however much they who marched South and
North in 1861 may have fixed on the technical points of union and local
autonomy as a shibboleth, all nevertheless knew, as we know, that the
question of Negro slavery was the real cause of the conflict. Curious it
was, too, how this deeper question ever forced itself to the surface despite
effort and disclaimer. No sooner had Northern armies touched Southern
soil than this old question, newly guised, sprang from the earth, —What
shall be done with Negroes? Peremptory military commands, this way
and that, could not answer the query; the Emancipation Proclamation
seemed but to broaden and intensify the difficulties; and the War Amendments[2] made the Negro problems of to-day.

Figure 2 *From* The Souls of Black Folk *(Bedford, 1997: 45), used with permission*

The combination of music and poetry also works to address Du Bois's concern about his book having too little emotional impact, which also might be indicated by his comment about a book of essays falling flat—falling flat, in other words, could mean failing to move readers. This seems like a valid concern, particularly given that some of the chapters of this book make relatively dry reading, Du Bois's often-poetic writing notwithstanding. Du Bois worried that the collections of facts typical of sociological studies could fail to be engaging. In one of his auto-biographies, for example, he characterized his doctor's thesis as "a dry historical treatise" that he had "succeeded in some degree" to make readable; he described his sociological study *The Philadelphia Negro* (1899) as "a huge volume of five hundred pages but not unreadable."[43] Given these lukewarm descriptions, it seems reasonable to assume that when he began to work on *Souls*, he was concerned about making sure the book had more impact on its reader.

Wagner came to believe that music was the most important form of art because it had the greatest ability to emotionally move its audience. If he was correct, the bars of song in *Souls* may have helped Du Bois enhance the book's emotional impact.[44] That is not to say that the essays play an insignificant role; instead, the combination of the intellectual understanding communicated by the essays and the emotional power of the music is essential to the effect of the whole. If "music was an emotional language that spoke directly, immediately to the feeling; while words addressed first the intellect and, if they were related to the feeling at all, only communicated to it at second hand," then ideally, when music and poetry were united, the intellectual and emotional appeals would reinforce and strengthen each other.[45]

But the question of the emotional impact of the music in *Souls* underlines the differences between *Souls* and Wagner's operas as total works of art. Of course, reading written notes from songs is a very different experience than hearing music performed, so it could reasonably be assumed that merely using the music as epigraphs in *Souls* wouldn't give the book the kind of impact Wagner achieved through performances of his operas. In other words, if Du Bois's songs remain silent markers—"hieroglyphs," as Cheryl Wall calls them[46]—it seems reason-

43. Du Bois, *Dusk of Dawn*, 269.

44. Wagner believed that music was "the voice of the heart" and that, among the arts, it had the greatest potential to move his audience to an understanding of "the inner essence of things." Berghaus, "A Theater," 16.

45. Glass, *The Fertilizing Seed*, 57.

46. Cheryl A. Wall, "Resounding *Souls*: Du Bois and the African American Literary Tradition," in this issue.

able to wonder if in fact they would have the kind of emotional impact Wagner attributed to music. But another of Wagner's ideas is that the impact of the arts depends on the engagement of the audience. Wagner believed that the message of the arts became fully realized only in the minds of the listeners—or, more likely, their hearts. In other words, a work of art depended in large part on the stimulation of the audience's imaginations; the full comprehension of the message of the work depended on "the active participation" of the audience members.[47] In that case, Du Bois's use of music is crucial in another way: it gets the reader actively engaged in his book. It is possible that when readers see the notes on the page, they might mentally sound them out; they might even try humming them. If they are familiar with the song, they might imagine the rest of it. If they do not recognize the songs or read music, it seems likely that the bars would at least spark their curiosity. Even if all they can do is ask questions about the notes, they are being engaged by the text. Their active response enhances the effect of the text.

If readers can sound out the music, that response gives the book a different kind of sensory appeal. The songs appeal to the reader orally, even if that sound has to be imagined. This was particularly the case for readers at the turn of the century who were familiar enough with the spirituals that the notes would have called to mind their texts and titles, even though Du Bois did not include the words.[48] In other words, the combination of music and poetry gives the book the kind of synesthetic effect that was one of the goals of the total work of art for the Romantics. This idea, too, has relevance to Du Bois's text: the possibility that Du Bois aimed at this kind of multisensory effect is suggested by the fact that he also used his prose to engage readers' senses. For example, Du Bois's description of the opera hall in the chapter about John appeals to four of our senses: John is awed by "the delicate beauty of the hall, the faint perfume, the moving myriad of men, the rich clothing and low hum of talking."[49] Elsewhere, Du Bois offered similarly evocative descriptions of the land, the communities he visited, and the people he met.

Reading *Souls* with the idea of synesthesia in mind also suggests that the different genres of writing in the book serve the purpose of appealing to readers in various ways. The book includes historical chapters, like "Of the Dawn of Freedom," where Du Bois recounted the events from 1861 to 1872, as well as sociological chapters, such as "Of the Black Belt," where he surveyed living con-

---

47. Berghaus, "A Theater," 14.
48. Sudquist, *To Wake the Nations*, 493, 531.
49. Du Bois, *Souls*, 176.

ditions for African Americans in Georgia. *Souls* also includes fiction in "Of the Coming of John"; personal reflection in "Of the Passing of the First Born," where Du Bois described the death of his first child; political argument in "Of Booker T. Washington and Others"; and cultural analysis in the final chapter, where he offered his reading of the sorrow songs. These different chapters appeal to readers intellectually but also emotionally: they inspire readers' imaginations as well as their understanding. It's not so much that the different genres of writing appeal to different senses, then, but that they appeal to different aspects of readers' intelligence. The combination of emotional and intellectual appeals in the various kinds of essays in *Souls*, in short, can be read as an application of Wagner's ideas to the forms of writing Du Bois had at his disposal as an author.

Such a reading of the book positions *Souls* as a total work of art that extends the boundaries of that idea as it had been formulated by Wagner. The nature of his book then allowed Du Bois to be more provocative than he might otherwise have been able to be. In other words, he could present arguments that challenged his readers because he had led them to a position in which they were already engaged. And, significantly, Du Bois's use of music feeds into one of the book's key arguments, which has to do with the evaluation of black culture. The combinations of music and poetry in *Souls* put the two forms of expression on par; they imply a degree of equivalence between the poems and the songs. This assertion of the value of the songs is a crucial part of Du Bois's reevaluation of black culture, which is most explicitly laid out in the book's final chapter. He described these "weird old songs" as "the articulate message of the slave to the world" and emphasized that they had a lasting and powerful impact on their hearers.[50] He pointed out that they "tell of death and suffering and unvoiced longing toward a truer world, of misty wanderings and hidden ways."[51] He gave examples of them moving soldiers to tears and quoted from scholars who assert their impact.[52] He also analyzed several of the songs, illuminating their hidden messages, their complexity, and their influence. In short, Du Bois showed the reader in this final essay that these spirituals were as expressive as poetry and, in fact, had a greater power to move their audiences than written words. The singing of African Americans "stirred men with a mighty power," as he wrote;[53] it is hard to imagine poetry as magical or as thrilling as the music Du Bois described.

50. Du Bois, *Souls*, 185, 187.
51. Du Bois, *Souls*, 187.
52. Du Bois, *Souls*, 188, 186, and 191.
53. Du Bois, *Souls*, 186.

In other words, Du Bois showed that the spirituals had all the complexity, themes, and impact of the canonical literature of the Western tradition. This is a crucial argument in the context of the early twentieth century, when the spirituals were more often assumed to be primitive, unrefined, and even childlike.[54] Du Bois, in fact, even hinted at this disparagement when he wrote in his final chapter that the spirituals had been "neglected," "half despised," and "persistently mistaken and misunderstood."[55] Du Bois, then, was enacting a major revision of the typical reception of the spirituals. But the fact that Du Bois set them on par with poetry is even more impressive given the high esteem generally given to poetry. The emphasis on European traditions in the schooling of many Americans taught them to value the tenants of Western culture: liberal education and individual accomplishments, especially as embodied in written literature. By the turn of the century, "certain moral and intellectual endeavors were designated the components of 'culture' and set apart from more functional aspects of society."[56] Poetry had long been understood as the highest of these high arts. Du Bois, then, was leading his readers to a reevaluation of America's cultural standards that reversed the assumptions they probably brought to *Souls*.

Du Bois's use of music also makes clear the limitations of the printed page, the privileged medium according to Western standards. To transcribe the songs into his book was a risky endeavor, because putting the spirituals onto paper fails in so many ways to capture their full complexity. Again, seeing the bars of music in the book is a very different experience than hearing music performed—but even this potential failure of music can be read as part of Du Bois's argument. The failure of Du Bois's transcriptions to be as effective as performed music serves rather than hinders his purposes. The presence of the songs gestures toward what is beyond the printed page, what cannot be captured in black and white, so to speak. The written versions of the spirituals fail to communicate so much about the songs. But in that final essay, Du Bois made clear that this was not a shortcoming of the music; it was a shortcoming of the printed page.

If what Du Bois showed were the limitations of the page, then an American culture that included only written texts was sorely lacking. And in fact, Du Bois emphasized that the spirituals represented the best of American music—and of American culture. He argued that American culture in general was lacking: "Lit-

54. Sundquist, *To Wake the Nations*, 477–79.
55. Du Bois, *Souls*, 186.
56. Houston A. Baker Jr., *Long Black Song: Essays in Black American Literature and Culture* (Charlottesville: University Press of Virginia, 1972), 5; for Baker's comments on Du Bois's revision of the Arnoldian definition of culture, see 106.

tle of beauty has America given the world save the rude grandeur God himself stamped on her bosom; the human spirit in this new world has expressed itself in vigor and ingenuity rather than in beauty."[57] The exception, of course, was the "Negro folk-song—the rhythmic cry of the slave," which, Du Bois wrote, "stands to-day not simply as the sole American music, but as the most beautiful expression of human experience born this side of the seas."[58] Even so, without analyses and explanations—like those Du Bois offered in his final chapter—the spirituals would not be fully understood or appreciated. What Du Bois set up, then, is a complex book in which none of the individual components would quite work on their own. Instead, to fully appreciate the messages of *Souls*, readers have to engage with music and writing in multiple forms. That complementary relationship serves as a metaphor, too, for Du Bois's understanding of American culture and even American society. He argued, after all, that his goal was not to "Africanize America, for America has too much to teach the world and Africa," but neither did he believe that an African American should "bleach his Negro soul . . . for he knows that Negro blood has a message for the world."[59] Instead, Du Bois asserted that both influences should be recognized and that the fullest American culture and society would come to fruition when the two could go hand in hand.

Of course, when *The Souls of Black Folk* was published, no one would have questioned the importance of white folk in America, and so it was the significance of African Americans that Du Bois had to emphasize. He ended the book with direct confrontations to his implicitly white readers: "Your country?" he demanded. "How came it [to be] yours? Before the Pilgrims landed we were here. Here we have brought our three gifts and mingled them with yours: a gift of story and song . . . the gift of sweat and brawn . . . [and] a gift of the Spirit."[60] Du Bois demonstrated those gifts throughout the book, in large part through the example of the songs. On that basis he was able to present a rhetorical question without needing to provide the answer: when he asked, "Would America have been America without her Negro people?," his readers have been taught that the answer is no.[61]

To read *Souls* through the model of Wagner's total work of art, then, is to discover the ways that the book recasts Wagner's ideas and techniques and applies them to African American culture and the struggle against racism. The fact that

57. Du Bois, *Souls*, 185–86.
58. Du Bois, *Souls*, 186.
59. Du Bois, *Souls*, 39.
60. Du Bois, *Souls*, 192–93.
61. Du Bois, *Souls*, 193.

Du Bois's mixture of texts is entirely in written form—that rather than heard music, sung poetry, and the movement of actors, Du Bois used transcribed bars of song and different forms of writing—marks *Souls* as a new kind of total work of art, a new form of creative and expository text hashed out to meet the demands of the unique situation of African Americans in America. It is ironic, though, that Wagner should have provided the model for Du Bois's efforts to battle American racism and discrimination, particularly given Wagner's own racism—or, more specifically, his anti-Semitism. Wagner's most notoriously anti-Semitic text is "Jewishness in Music" (1850). Like many of his fellow German nationalists, Wagner argued that Jews were essentially un-German and that the unification of the nation depended upon exclusion of the Jews. Wagner used familiar anti-Semitic stereotypes in his essay when he maligned Jews and attacked the work of Jewish composers as derivative.[62] Du Bois, who experienced so much racism firsthand, was "averse to stereotypes 'from principle.'"[63] Furthermore, Wagner's arguments against Jews paralleled those used against African Americans in the United States. Wagner's arguments for racial purity and national exclusiveness were antithetical to Du Bois's arguments for the integration of African Americans into American society and for his understanding of the cultural pluralism of American culture. For these reasons, Du Bois's admiration of Wagner is surprising. As a member of a persecuted minority in the United States, Du Bois's goal was to promote national unity based on inclusion, not exclusion. Wagner's concept of national identity, in short, was strikingly different from Du Bois's. The fact that Du Bois used Wagner's formal innovations in pursuit of such radically different ideals testifies to the adaptability of the idea of the total work of art as well as to Du Bois's innovativeness.

62. Barry Millington, "Wagner and the Jews," in Millington, *The Wagner Compendium*, 161–64. Wagner's ideas were famously appropriated and echoed by Hitler and the Nazis in the twentieth century, and Wagner's work was used as "theme music for the Third Reich." David C. Large, "Posthumous Reputation and Influence," in Millington, *The Wagner Compendium*, 389. For extensive discussion, see Leon Stein, *The Racial Thinking of Richard Wagner* (New York: Philosophical Library, 1950), as well as Paul Lawrence Rose, *Wagner: Race and Revolution* (New Haven, Conn.: Yale University Press, 1992).

63. Lewis, *W. E. B. Du Bois*, 148. Anti-Semitism did sometimes creep into his own work, though. David Blight and Robert Gooding-Williams note that *Souls* was not free of anti-Semitic comments but also that Du Bois purged most of these comments from the 1953 edition of the book. See Du Bois, *Souls*, 266 and 209–10n20. In columns he wrote for the *Pittsburgh Courier*, Du Bois also commented critically on anti-Semitism in Germany during a visit to that country in 1936. He described his visits to Bayreuth, asserted the relevance of Wagner's operas to the struggles of African Americans, and critiqued the discrimination carried out against the Jews. See the columns of various titles published from October 31, 1936, through January 2, 1937, under the headline "Forum of Fact and Opinion," reprinted in Du Bois, *Newspaper Columns*, 124–56.

But Du Bois's creation of a text that unifies music and poetry, in a sense, is even more appropriate to Wagner's ideals than Wagner's own operas. If a total work of art unifies texts in different media, it enacts the same process of blending as does a pluralistic national culture. Just as in the *Gesamtkunstwerk*, where the works in different media are unified into a whole that transcends the meaning of the parts, so American society might transcend the potential of its parts when black and white citizens are brought together into a unified national whole. Of course, in 1903, this idea was far into the future—another way that Du Bois's creation follows Wagner's model, for Wagner believed that the fully realized total work of art would only be achieved in the years to come, as the title "Art-Work of the Future" suggests. The fact that Du Bois, not Wagner, was able to imagine an artwork of the future that would not only blend various media but also embody a racially inclusive national culture and society is a testament to Du Bois's vision.

Overall, then, Du Bois turned *Souls* into a provocative total work of art that capitalizes on and extends Wagner's concept of the form. We could argue that Du Bois's combination of music and poetry unifies and enhances his book even without Wagner's ideas in mind, but to consider *Souls* in the context of Wagner's influence and the development of ideas about the unity of the arts underlines the innovative formal and conceptual qualities of the book. Furthermore, to read *Souls* in this context deepens our appreciation of Du Bois's skills as a writer. Most important, seeing *Souls* as an example of the kind of total work of art encouraged by Wagner identifies Du Bois as an intellectual who was influenced by art theory and who was quite successful in applying wide-ranging ideas about the relations between the arts to his representation of life on the color line. In other words, it shows Du Bois to be someone who was able to appropriate sophisticated theories about the ways texts worked and to use them toward his own goal of changing how his readers understood African Americans' lives and experiences.

Reading *Souls* in this way also reminds us how important the arts were to Du Bois. Of course, he was trained as a sociologist and a historian and was deeply involved in efforts to bring about social change. Simultaneously, though, he also was very interested in and moved by ideas about the arts, and he found ways to incorporate the arts into his struggle for civil rights and equality for African Americans. That is true of *Souls* but also of his work in the decades after he wrote this book. The kinds of connections among the arts present in *Souls* are also evident, for example, in the pageant he developed about ten years after *Souls*. In its most polished version, it was called "The Star of Ethiopia," and it was an elaborate theatrical event that included music, actors, and dramatic stage sets; it thus brought together work in many different media.[64] Du Bois's work in the 1910s and the 1920s, particularly as editor of *The Crisis*, offers many other examples of his use of different kinds of art to undermine racism. In his essays, Du Bois often discussed music, visual images, and performances, along with literature; contests run in the 1920s by *The Crisis* included categories for many various types of art; and often poems and short stories were illustrated when they were published in the magazine.[65] In short, *The Crisis* became another example of the kind of total work of art for which Wagner called.

The echoes of Wagner in *Souls*, then, draw attention to Du Bois's continuing strategy of fusing the arts in his efforts to fight racism. Du Bois, clearly, was an activist who used any and all tools at his disposal. To fully appreciate the magnitude of his intellect and his accomplishments, we need to continue to explore the full range of the allusions in his work and to enhance our sensitivities to its scope. In return, we discover new ways that his oeuvre speaks to our own struggles against racism. Du Bois continues to inspire us to create new kinds of work that might advance our efforts for social justice.

Anne E. Carroll teaches American and African American literature in the English department at Wichita State University. She is the author of *Word, Image, and the New Negro: Representation and Identity in the Harlem Renaissance* (2005) as well as numerous published essays. She is also an associate editor of and contributor to *The Encyclopedia of the Harlem Renaissance* (2004).

64. For discussion of the development of the pageant, which was first staged in 1913 and then toured a number of cities in 1915, see Lewis, *W. E. B. Du Bois*, 459–61.

65. Anne Elizabeth Carroll, *Word, Image, and the New Negro: Representation and Identity in the Harlem Renaissance* (Bloomington: Indiana University Press, 2005), especially chap. 3.

Queering *The Souls of Black Folk*

Charles I. Nero

In 1890, W. E. B. Du Bois delivered "Jefferson Davis as Representative of Civilization" as his Harvard commencement address. According to David Levering Lewis, a biographer of Du Bois, the young scholar was greeted by an avalanche of positive reactions from the national press for a "brilliant and eloquent address."[1] It was ironic that the African American Du Bois speaking before a New England audience selected Davis, the former president of the Confederacy, as his representative of civilization. "In choosing Davis," Shamoon Zamir writes, Du Bois selected "the leader of the defeated and racist South, a figure heavy with symbolic resonance and the memory of national division, as the logical telos of an unself-conscious New England idealism, and that at a time of rising nationalism."[2] Yet this irony allowed Du Bois to intervene in the public culture of white supremacy after Reconstruction with a message that was calibrated "to flatter as carefully as any address ever given by Booker T. Washington before a white audience."[3] Du Bois proposed a new, post-Reconstruction America formed through a patriarchal union of white and black men. A decade later, in the face of seemingly

The author gratefully acknowledges the support and helpful comments from audience members at Northwestern University's "100 Years of *The Souls of Black Folk*" conference, Dwight McBride, Robert Gooding-Williams, Sue E. Houchins, Paul Outlaw, and especially Baltasar Fra-Molinero.

1. David Levering Lewis, *W. E. B. Du Bois—Biography of a Race, 1868–1919* (New York: Holt, 1993), 101.

2. Shamoon Zamir, *Dark Voices: W. E. B. Du Bois and American Thought, 1888–1903* (Chicago: University of Chicago Press, 1995), 63.

3. Lewis, *W. E. B. Du Bois—Biography of a Race*, 102.

Public Culture 17(2): 255–76

intractable racism, Du Bois announced his retreat from his earlier idealism in "Of the Coming of John," the lone short story in his 1903 classic, *Souls of Black Folk*. Originally, the story was to be the final chapter of *Souls*; however, at the suggestion of his publishers, Du Bois added a chapter about Negro spirituals at the end of the book.[4] This new chapter emphasized African cultural retentions among black Americans, their spirituality and their endurance. In effect, this new chapter blunted Du Bois's political message by deflecting attention away from "Of the Coming of John"'s significant revision of the idealism he had expressed in "Jefferson Davis."

This essay examines the revision of the Harvard speech in "Of the Coming of John." It pays particular attention to violence as the expression of Du Bois's disillusionment with an America redeemed through *biracial* male partnership. I argue that the biracial male union Du Bois represented in his Harvard address is impossible because of the rigid policing of sexual identity categories at the turn of the century. This argument does not deny that the hardening of racism would have produced disillusionment from Du Bois; rather, it follows Siobhan Somerville's observation that at the end of the nineteenth century, "as racialized boundaries were increasingly policed, so too were emerging categories of sexual identity." Especially relevant is Somerville's argument that "negotiations of the color line . . . shaped and were shaped by the emergence of notions of sexual identity and the corresponding epistemological uncertainties surrounding them."[5] "Of the Coming of John" is a text bloated with epistemological uncertainties as Du Bois charts his central character's movement from a peasant to what Houston Baker calls "a tragic black man of culture who is not accepted by whites and who is too elevated to communicate with his own people—'the ignorant and turbulent' black proletariat."[6]

My readings of both the short story and the earlier speech call attention to queer meanings that I believe are inherent in these texts. Here, I am not using *queer* in the sense used by middle-class men in the 1910s and 1920s to identify "themselves as different from other men primarily on the basis of heir homosexual interest."[7] Instead, I follow Anne Herrmann's suggestion that for modernists,

4. A. S. McClurg and Company to W. E. B. Du Bois, Chicago, January 21, 1903, in *The Papers of W. E. B. Du Bois, 1803 (1877–1963) 1965* (Sanford, N.C.: Microfilming Corporation of America, 1981), reel 2, frame 433.

5. Siobhan B. Somerville, *Queering the Color Line: Race and the Invention of Homosexuality in American Culture* (Durham, N.C.: Duke University Press, 2000), 2, 3.

6. Houston A. Baker Jr., *Long Black Song: Essays in Black American Literature and Culture* (Charlottesville: University of Virginia Press, 1972), 102.

7. George Chauncey, *Gay New York: Gender, Urban Culture, and the Making of the Gay Male World, 1890–1940* (New York: Basic Books, 1994), 101.

"queerness is less about object choice than about the recognition on the part of others that one is not like others, a subject out of order, not in sequence, not working." Herrmann sees in the term *queer* a "resistance to regimes of the normal" by "not changing identities to justify desire, but desiring in ways that make strange the relations between identities."[8] Although I am developing a queer analysis in this essay, I should also make it clear that my approach is complementary—rather than oppositional—to analyses, in particular feminist ones, that contest masculinity as natural. I am thinking in particular of Hazel Carby's discovery in *Souls* of "an anxiety of masculinity . . . embedded in the landscape of a crisis in the social order." The queer reading in this essay pays attention to what Carby identifies as the "process of gendering" in *Souls* that allows Du Bois to make "distinctions within his definition of masculinity itself."[9]

I contend that in "Of the Coming of John," Du Bois is troubled by the meaning of a union between black and white men that was structurally impossible in the early-twentieth-century United States. The authority of men to exchange women among one another is crucial to the argument I make here about equality. Eve Kosofsky Sedgwick follows the classical anthropological work of Claude Lévi-Strauss, who defines culture in terms of a "total relationship of exchange . . . not established between a man and a woman, but between two groups of men, [in which] the woman figures only as one of the objects in the exchange, not as one of the partners."[10] This transaction of women forms a homosocial contract between men which is culture. What troubles Du Bois in "Of the Coming of John" is that miscegenation laws make the legitimate exchange of women across racial borders impossible. Moreover, as sexual identity boundaries are being policed, the basis for biracial union requires that black men assume a stigmatized identity. In "Of the Coming of John," Du Bois produces a text that records his anxieties, or "epistemological uncertainties" to use Somerville's term, about emerging conceptions of normalcy that govern male bonding and the formation of patriarchal nationalism in the early twentieth century.

8. Anne Herrmann, *Queering the Moderns: Poses/Portraits/Performances* (New York: Palgrave, 2000), 6–7.

9. Hazel V. Carby, *Race Men* (Cambridge, Mass.: Harvard University Press, 1998), 28, 30.

10. Eve Kosofsky Sedgwick, *Epistemology of the Closet* (Berkeley: University of California Press, 1990), 184.

A Nation Redeemed By Male Desire

In "Jefferson Davis as a Representative of Civilization," Du Bois presented his view of an America redeemed from the chaos of the Civil War by a homosocial and patriarchal formula.[11] This formula required balancing the best qualities from white and black males: "Jefferson Davis was a typical Teutonic Hero," the embodiment of "the Strong Man," Du Bois declared, a "soldier and a lover, a statesman and a ruler; passionate, ambitious and indomitable; bold reckless guardian." Davis was undeniably "noble"; yet, Du Bois stated, if Davis were "judged by every canon of human justice," he would be seen as "fundamentally incomplete." Du Bois made it clear that Davis represented not only a man but "the type of civilization which his life represented." Although this civilization "represents a field for stalwart manhood and heroic character," Du Bois charged that it simultaneously represents "moral obtuseness and refined brutality." In a dialectical manner Du Bois argued that the Submissive Man was a natural balance for the Strong Man; for civilization to advance, the Strong Man must heed the advice of the Submissive Man. Du Bois proclaimed that "civilization cannot afford to lose the contribution of the very least of nations for its full development" because "not only the assertion of the I, but also the submission of the Thou is the highest individualism."[12]

Clearly, Du Bois understood submission as a positive trait. The problem, he explained, is that submission only had negative connotations of "cowardice, laziness or stupidity," and Du Bois proposed replacing these with the idea that the Submissive Man "was the personification of dogged patience bending to the inevitable, and waiting."[13] Zamir explains that Du Bois was proposing "a kind of Christian-Hegelian recognition of duty and collective debt as the basis of the state—not subservience."[14] When Du Bois identified African Americans as the model for this idea of submission, he was following a tradition popularized by nineteenth-century abolitionists that invested African Americans with the ideals of American Christian messianism.[15] Du Bois made this tradition evident in the supplication that closes his address, "You owe a debt to humanity for this Ethiopia

---

11. W. E. B. Du Bois, "Jefferson Davis as a Representative of Civilization," in *The Oxford W. E. B. Du Bois Reader*, ed. Eric J. Sundquist (New York: Oxford University Press, 1996), 242–43.

12. Du Bois, "Jefferson Davis," 243–44.

13. Du Bois, "Jefferson Davis," 244.

14. Zamir, *Dark Voices*, 64.

15. Wilson Jeremiah Moses, *Black Messiahs and Uncle Toms: Social and Literary Manipulations of a Religious Myth* (University Park: Pennsylvania State University Press, 1993), especially chaps. 4 and 5.

of the Outstretched Arm, who has made her beauty, patience, and her grandeur law."[16] This allusion to the biblical prophecy in the Psalms (68:31) that "Ethiopia shall soon stretch out her hands unto God!" represents what many nineteenth-century African and Anglo-American Christians believed was eventually "the destiny of black people to create an exemplary civilization" either in Africa or elsewhere.[17]

This manifest destiny to build a great civilization could only be achieved through a union of the Teutonic Strong Man and the African Submissive Man. Du Bois stated: "The Teuton stands today as the champion of the idea of Personal Assertion: the Negro as the peculiar embodiment of the idea of Personal Submission: either, alone, tends to an abnormal development—towards Despotism on the one hand which the world has just cause to fear, and yet covertly admires, or towards slavery on the other which the world despises and which yet is not wholly despicable."[18] As Zamir points out, this was a further irony in which Du Bois made his own "representative maneuver" in a speech putatively about white heroes.[19]

The fact should not be lost on us that Du Bois's language for imagining this union between white and black men is unusually inflected by gender. The African American is the representative of, Du Bois wrote, an "effete civilization," while the "great and striking" Teuton embodies "impetuous manhood."[20] That Du Bois imagines the nation as collaboration among men should not surprise us. Writing in a different context about opera and male desire, Wayne Koestenbaum remarks that "it's no coincidence that the phonograph was invented by men in collaboration, for there are many cases of nineteenth-century writers or scientists collaborating in order to control and impersonate mysteries imagined to be feminine and reproductive."[21] Not surprisingly, Du Bois's ideal of collaboration of black and white males draws on the language of reproduction. The Teutonic Strong Man and the African Submissive Man strive for union which leads to a pregnancy that Du Bois calls a "round and full development."[22] Du Bois will appropriate

16. Du Bois, "Jefferson Davis," 245.

17. Wilson Jeremiah Moses, *The Wings of Ethiopia: Studies in African-American Life and Letters* (Ames: Iowa State University Press, 1990), 102–3.

18. Du Bois, "Jefferson Davis," 245.

19. Zamir, *Dark Voices*, 64.

20. Du Bois, "Jefferson Davis," 245.

21. Wayne Koestenbaum, *The Queen's Throat: Opera, Homosexuality, and the Mystery of Desire* (New York: Poseidon, 1993), 49.

22. Du Bois, "Jefferson Davis," 245.

the feminine again as a means of furthering biracial male cooperation in "Of the Coming of John."

The idealism Du Bois expressed in his 1890 speech was difficult to sustain over the next decade. Antiblack racism became more intractable as years passed. The U.S. Supreme Court case of *Plessy v. Ferguson* (1896) and its separate-but-equal ruling made segregation the law of the land. The southern states passed laws that disenfranchised African Americans, while lynch law and terrorism effectively removed African Americans from holding local public offices. By 1900 African Americans had lost all of the political gains made during Reconstruction. The rise of white violence and racism toward blacks in the United States was an inescapable fact that Du Bois could not ignore. "Of the Coming of John" is a record of violence that significantly revises the idealism of biracial male homosocial desire as the foundation for national unity that Du Bois expressed in his Harvard speech.

"Of the Coming of John"

"Of the Coming of John," notes Arnold Rampersad, "elaborates the duality of the black soul."[23] There are two Johns in the story. The black John, John Jones, struggles at school, while the white John is the privileged son of Judge Henderson, the main citizen of the small Georgia town where both Johns live. The black and white worlds think only of their favorite sons. Playmates in childhood, the young men go away to school, and both return dissatisfied. White John is bored by small-town life. John Jones returns a brooding figure, Rampersad writes, a "would-be black *savant* caught in a dilemma between two worlds."[24] Judge Henderson fires Jones from his position as teacher in the local black school. Wandering in a daze, he comes upon the white John Henderson, who is attempting to rape Jones's sister, and finally kills his double. John Jones faces the Atlantic Ocean and waits for what appears to be a lynch mob, calmly accepting his death.

Clearly, violence is a central motif for this story, and it is especially meaningful in three pivotal moments in the story that play up Du Bois's disillusionment about racial union in post-Reconstruction America. The first two incidents, which occur in New York City, demonstrate the enforcement of a racial caste system in which whites must be prepared to suppress with violence any act of nondeferential behavior from blacks. In the first, Jones accidentally brushes against Henderson while the two share the democratic space of a ticket line outside an

23. Arnold Rampersad, *The Art and Imagination of W. E. B. Du Bois* (New York: Schocken, 1990), 75.
24. Rampersad, *Art and Imagination*, 75.

opera house where Richard Wagner's *Lohengrin* is being performed. Henderson's white female date hints at his annoyance—possibly verging on violence—when she teasingly remarks, "You must not lynch the colored man, simply because he is in your way."[25] Later, inside the opera house, Jones finds himself seated next to Henderson's escort. Inadvertently, John touches the date's arm and she recoils. Lynching is still out of the question; however, Henderson does manage to have Jones evicted from the theater during the overture.

The third act of violence is real, not imagined. John Henderson has returned from Princeton to his home in Altamaha and is clearly bored in a "God-forgotten town" that has nothing to offer but "mud and Negroes."[26] To amuse himself, Henderson exercises his privilege as the son of an upper-class white southern family by raping a young black female servant—Jennie, who as it happens is the sister of John Jones. When Jennie extricates herself from her assailant, he follows her into the woods. Upon seeing his sister in struggle, John picks up a fallen tree limb and beats to the death his sister's assailant and his double. Facing the Atlantic Ocean, John hums the "Song of the Bride" from Wagner's *Lohengrin* as he waits for what appears to be a lynch mob led by Judge Henderson.

Eric Sundquist suggests that this melodramatic ending, with its reference to Wagner's opera, is an example of double consciousness. Sundquist pays particular attention to the musical quotation at the beginning of the story, the spiritual "When the Trumpet Sounds," also known as "You May Bury Me in the East." According to Sundquist, this spiritual alludes "to a central legend of African tradition that survived in the slaves' folk belief that they might one day fly home to Africa," but additionally, Du Bois uses it to relate Wagner to African American experience:

> The spiritual offers an African American version of the act of Transcendence that Du Bois borrows from the figure of the swan, translating martial power into Romantic idealism, at the conclusion of Wagner's opera. In this story of cultural doublings, the sounding trumpet of resurrection in the spiritual is appropriately doubled in the Wagnerian brass that accompanies the climax of *Lohengrin*. The two pieces of music therefore stand in a relationship that is not unlike that of the two Johns—the one black, the other white—whose contrasting lives are shown in the story to be the products of racist society.[27]

25. W. E. B. Du Bois, *The Souls of Black Folk*, ed. David W. Blight and Robert Gooding-Williams (1903; Boston: St. Martin's, 1997), 176. All subsequent references to *The Souls of Black Folk* are to this edition.

26. Du Bois, *Souls*, 181.

27. Eric J. Sundquist, *To Wake the Nations: Race in the Making of American Literature* (Cambridge, Mass.: Harvard University Press, 1993), 523.

Sundquist's powerful analysis affirms a racial reading for "Of the Coming of John," since the story points out how race—and race alone—determines the tragic fate of two young men from the same town.

The acts of real and imagined violence in the story show that racial distinctions and their enforcement make it impossible for black and white men to form a union. Viewed this way, the story is a tragic indictment of the maintenance and enforcement of racial differences. Black and white men can never establish a nation together contra Du Bois's prophesy in "Jefferson Davis." Returning to Sedgwick, we recall that the exchange of women is what binds men's relationships to one another.[28] However, white men are not obligated to respect black men, and *Souls* shows that they may rape black women with impunity in the turn-of-the-century American South. By contrast, white men interpret any sexual interest by black men toward white women as a justification for violence. In other words, union between black and white men is impossible since neither can give to the other the gift of a woman. In fact, the rape of Jennie shows that John's gift of a woman would be redundant since Henderson already has access to her.

Here Comes the Bride

Scholars seem reluctant to discuss Du Bois's use of "The Song of the Bride" (known more popularly in English as "Here Comes the Bride"), and existing analyses have ended up affirming only a racial reading of the story. Sundquist, for instance, pays attention to the choice of Wagner, not the specific song, when he states that the music is a "reminder of John's humiliation at a New York concert when his white double forces him out of the theater; more broadly, it is a reminder, as it was for Du Bois, that his intellect and his aspirations, no matter their power, would be judged not fit for European American high culture simply because of his color."[29] Sundquist's comment is problematic insofar as it avoids discussing the specific song; Du Bois could have chosen any piece from *Lohengrin* to indicate the racial dilemma. In the most sustained discussion of Wagner and Du Bois to date, Russell Berman also privileges a racial reading of the story when he pays attention to the song chosen but uses a rather heterosexist premise to reach the conclusion that Du Bois recovers a dormant democratic impulse in Wagner. For Berman, "The Song of the Bride" calls attention to Du Bois's "desire for a race-

28. Sedgwick, *Epistemology of the Closet*, 184.
29. Sundquist, *To Wake the Nations*, 521.

blind love" that is a necessary component for a democracy.[30] This gesture toward democracy is consistent with the "Jefferson Davis" speech; however, Berman overreaches when he makes the desire in the story heterosexual, suggesting that Du Bois's choice of "The Bridal Song" is an autobiographical reflection. Berman argues that Du Bois is referring to a love affair the young scholar had with a white woman during his stay in Germany in 1892. The problem with Berman's reading the story as autobiographical is that John Jones expresses no heterosexual desire in the short story. Thus, Berman's heterosexualizing of John seems at best like normativizing desire and policing it at worst.

A likely cause of the difficulty critics have with "The Song of the Bride" may be that the story's narrator is classically unreliable. When Wagner's "Song of the Bride" occurs, the narrator says that John "is softly humming" the song. There are two significant issues about this moment that underscore such unreliability and, I believe, support a queer reading of the story. First, the narrator does not tell us how John comes to learn "The Song of the Bride." John could not have heard it in the opera house, since he was asked to leave the theater during the overture and "the Song of the Bride" does not occur until the third act. It seems more likely that this music is used much like a film sound track's nondiegetic score; that is, music that the audience hears but that the characters in the film do not. Often, this music serves to comment on a character's interiority or state of mind. In this case, then, I suggest the music comments on John's female interiority as the bride.

Second, John is "softly humming" the song, but the narrator contradicts this when its lyrics are provided. Furthermore, the lyrics the narrator provides are incorrect: "*Freudig geführt, ziehet dahin.*" In fact, the actual lyrics are "*Treulich geführt, ziehet dahin,*" which means "Faithfully or Loyally led, draw near." Instead of "Faithfully/Loyally," the narrator changes the lyrics to "Joyfully" (*Freudig*). Critics have usually paid little attention to this change, suggesting, as Russell Berman does, that it is an understandable mistake for one who is not a native speaker of German. But there is strong evidence that this mistake was intentional. For one thing, Du Bois never corrected the text in subsequent editions even though, as Henry Louis Gates Jr. has shown, Du Bois made "subtle" changes to *The Souls of Black Folk* so long as they did not alter the pagination in the twenty-four editions published between 1903 and 1953.[31] Surely, changing *Freudig* to *Treulich* would not have been difficult.

30. Russell A. Berman, "Du Bois and Wagner: Race, Nation, and Culture between the United States and Germany," *German Quarterly* 70 (1997): 130.

31. Henry Louis Gates Jr., "Introduction," in *The Souls of Black Folk*, by W. E. B. Du Bois (1903; New York: Bantam, 1989), xxv.

A more important clue lies in a 1936 *Pittsburg Courier* column "Opera and the Negro Problem," in which Du Bois repeated the mistranslation in "Of the Coming of John." The fact that Du Bois made this mistake some thirty years later is noteworthy, since he considered *Lohengrin* his favorite opera, having "heard it six or eight times, under many circumstances, in different languages and lands," Du Bois wrote. Actually, the 1936 column reveals that Du Bois had a well-thought analysis of the opera that depended upon the substitution of "Joyfully" for "Loyally/Faithfully": "It all waits on that unforgettable hymn of the bride, without which it is difficult for a woman to feel really married—Freudig gefuert, wiehet dahin." Metaphorically, the bride's entry into marriage was evidence for "something in this world man must trust" because, Du Bois wrote, "One cannot live and doubt everybody and everything. Somewhere in this world and not beyond it, there is Trust, and somehow Trust leads to Joy."[32] Du Bois's analysis privileges Joy. What I am suggesting is that the substitution of "Joyfully" for "Faithfully/Loyally" is consistent with Du Bois's depiction of John as the ideal of the Submissive Man. John approaches the act of submission much as a bride approaches her husband on the wedding day. The act is done with a faith or loyalty that leads ultimately to the higher state that Du Bois called "Joy."

Why is Du Bois appropriating a feminine concept, *the bride*, for his male character John Jones? Sedgwick's analysis of William Wycherley's Restoration comedy *The Country Wife* (1675) is helpful. Also, it allows us to understand how "Of the Coming of John" responds to the policing of gender and sexuality at the turn of the century. Two noteworthy points emerge in Sedgwick's analysis. First, when men misunderstand "the kind of property women are or the kind of transaction in which alone their value is realizable means," men risk becoming cuckolds; that is, they risk becoming "permanently feminized or objectified in relation to other men." Second, the successful transaction of women, Sedgwick states, requires from men "a willingness and ability to temporarily risk, or assume a feminized status."[33] Sedgwick's comments allows for a greater explication of the desire underlying "Jefferson Davis" and of its frustration in "Of the Coming of John."

I submit that John Jones assumes the feminine position that Sedgwick identifies as necessary for men's entitlement through transactions of women as symbolic currency. John Jones becomes the feminine figure in "The Bridal March." However, when Du Bois enacts John Jones's assumption of femininity, it is now

32. W. E. B. Du Bois, "Opera and the Negro Problem," *Pittsburgh Courier*, October 31, 1936, sec. 2.

33. Eve Kosofsky Sedgwick, *Between Men: English Literature and Male Homosocial Desire* (New York: Columbia University Press, 1985), 51.

tainted by a stigmatized identity called "gender inversion," a scientific theory from the late nineteenth century that Du Bois could have encountered through his academic study in either Germany or in the United States. Inversion theories first developed in Germany in 1864, when Karl Heinrich Ulrichs used the terms *Urning* and *Uranism* to describe "a female psyche confined in a male body."[34] By the 1880s and 1890s articles about *Urnings*, *Uranism*, *sexual inversion*, and another popular term, *contrary sexual feelings*, were appearing in American medical journals.[35]

Inversion theories played a key role in the development of modern sexual identity theories, since sexologists imagined that homosexual desire emerged when a body contained the psyche of the other gender because it was believed that all desire was essentially heterosexual. Historian Jonathan Ned Katz contends that the end of the nineteenth century "represents the first years of the heterosexual epoch," in which "doctors of the mind . . . first publicly formulated the idea of *heterosexual* and *homosexual*."[36] This "invention" marked the creation of modern homophobia and the homosexual as the deviant counterpart of the healthy, natural heterosexual. The development and widespread belief in homosexual identity would have a profound impact on the homosocial bonds that regulated male gender. The development of "the heterosexual epoch" is significant not only for a secular, scientific basis for persecuting homosexual men, but also "for the regulation of the male homosocial bonds that structure . . . all public or heterosexual culture." Sedgwick writes that "the paths of male entitlement, especially in the nineteenth century, required certain intense male bonds that were not readily distinguishable from the most reprobated bonds, an endemic and ineradicable state of . . . male homosexual panic became the normal condition of male heterosexual entitlement."[37] Viewed in this way, the nineteenth-century culture of public heterosexuality uses homophobia to regulate the bonds between men for entitlement and power. Of course, the regulation of these bonds creates a coercive double bind, as Sedgwick writes in *Between Men*: "For a man to be a man's man is separated only by an invisible carefully blurred, always-already crossed line from being 'interested in men.' "[38] Du Bois's black protagonist is caught in this double bind.

---

34. Hubert Kennedy, "Karl Heinrich Ulrichs, First Theorist of Homosexuality," in *Science and Homosexualities*, ed. Vernon Rosario (New York: Routledge, 1997), 29.

35. Somerville, *Queering the Color Line*, 18–33.

36. Jonathan Ned Katz, *The Invention of Heterosexuality* (New York: Dutton, 1995), 32.

37. Sedgwick, *Epistemology of the Closet*, 184–85.

38. Sedgwick, *Between Men*, 89.

Gender inversion is wholly consistent with the concept of the Submissive Man that Du Bois first described in "Jefferson Davis" and later attributes to his protagonist in "Of the Coming of John." Du Bois makes this attribution to John by a connection between Submissiveness and the Judeo-Christian tradition. In this particular case, we see Du Bois once again appropriating the feminine for masculine uses. Du Bois associates John with an undisputedly feminine, messianic character.

Du Bois Appropriates Queen Esther

John's moment of gender inversion occurs after he accepts his messianic duty to return to Altamaha. John directly quotes the words of the Old Testament's Queen Esther: "I will go in to the King, which is not according to law; and if I perish, I perish."[39] Here John is "voice merging" with the biblical queen, a practice in which those with a sacred duty fuse their voices with the authority derived from biblical characters.[40] By voice merging, John both legitimates his future activities as doing the work of God and bestows upon himself the authority that a community of believers endows upon its prophets. John's voice merging with the biblical Queen Esther requires attention, for "when we do not recognize allusions to specific Bible verses, stories, characters, images or words," critics of African American literature "often underread or misunderstand the references and implications of individual texts and the patterns and contexts of their authors."[41] "Of the Coming of John" is continually underread when critics ignore Queen Esther and pay attention only to allusions to male messianic figures in the text, such as John the Baptist, Jesus Christ, Moses, or Wagner's Lohengrin.

Queen Esther was a well-known figure in nineteenth- and early-twentieth-century black America through the efforts of African American women who repeatedly referred to her to legitimate their participation in public life. Maria Stewart, "America's first black woman political writer," and the first woman of any race in the United States whose public speeches were published, drew on the figure of Queen Esther to challenge the prevailing sexist customs that forbade women from engaging in public speaking.[42] In an address delivered in Boston

39. Du Bois, *Souls*, 178.
40. Keith Miller, "Voice Merging and Self-Making: The Epistemology of 'I Have a Dream,'" *Rhetoric Society Quarterly* 19 (1989): 23–31.
41. Frances Smith Foster and Chanta Haywood, "Christian Recordings: Afro-Protestantism, Its Press, and the Production of African-American Literature," *Religion and Literature* 27 (1995): 17.
42. Marilyn Richardson, *Maria W. Stewart: America's First Black Woman Political Writer* (Bloomington: Indiana University Press, 1987).

on September 21, 1833, on the subject of abolition and her right to speak about it, Stewart asked her astonished audience, "What if I am a woman; is not the God of ancient times the God to these modern days? . . . Did not Queen Esther save the lives of the Jews?"[43] We find references to Queen Esther in the speeches of Sojourner Truth,[44] the poetry and novels of Frances Ellen Watkins Harper,[45] the political writings of black club women at the turn of the century,[46] the musical choices of black women classical singers,[47] and the activism of black church women.[48] One of the highest compliments that African American Baptist women paid to the antilynching crusade of Ida B. Wells was that we have "found in our race a queen Esther, a woman of high talent, that has sounded the bugle for a defenseless race."[49]

Clearly, John's voice merging with that of Queen Esther would have been meaningful to a biblically literate and politically conscious reading culture at the beginning of the twentieth century. That John quoted Queen Esther to legitimate his future action is, I dare say, a queer choice. It aligns his male protagonist with a socially feminized text. Moreover, Queen Esther is truly a minority text, since it is only one of two books of the Bible in which a female is the protagonist. One must wonder why Du Bois would choose Queen Esther for such a pivotal moment in the story when he could select from the entire panoply of male prophets from the Bible. Why would Du Bois choose Esther, a book that has been controversial since Martin Luther reviled it for being "heathen" and for its excessive "judaizing"?[50]

43. Maria W. Stewart, "What If I Am a Woman?" in *Lift Every Voice: African American Oratory, 1787–1900*, ed. Philip S. Finer and Robert Branham (Baton Rouge: Louisiana State University Press, 1998), 138.

44. Entry on Sojourner Truth in *Black Women in White America: A Documentary History*, ed. Gerda Lerner (New York: Pantheon, 1972), 567–68.

45. Frances Ellen Watkins Harper, "Vashti," in *A Brighter Coming Day: A Frances Ellen Watkins Harper Reader*, ed. Frances Smith Foster (New York: Feminist Press, 1990), 182; Frances Ellen Watkins Harper, *Iola Leroy; or, Shadows Uplifted* (1893; New York: Oxford University Press, 1988), 75.

46. Lillian S. Williams, "Mary Morris Talbert," in *Notable Black American Women*, ed. Jessie Carney Smith (Detroit, Mich.: Gale, 1992), 1097.

47. Juanita Karpf, "'As with Words of Fire': Art Music and Nineteenth-Century African American Feminist Discourse," *Signs: Journal of Women in Culture and Society* 24 (1999): 603–33.

48. Evelyn Brooks Higginbotham, *Righteous Discontent: The Women's Movement in the Black Baptist Church, 1880–1920* (Cambridge, Mass.: Harvard University Press, 1993), 143.

49. Higginbotham, *Righteous Discontent*, 143.

50. Elias Joseph Bickerman, *Four Strange Books of the Bible: Jonah, Daniel, Koheleth, Esther* (New York: Schocken, 1967), 212.

Esther is a motif in "Of the Coming of John" that critics have overlooked. An incident on Du Bois's twenty-fifth birthday in Germany is illustrative. On that occasion Du Bois engaged in a feast of eating and drinking that is not unlike the carnival the Talmud encourages for Purim celebrations. At midnight Du Bois wrote in a notebook:

> I rejoice as a strong man to run a race, and I am strong—is it egotism—is it assurance—or is it the silent call of the world spirit that makes me feel that I am royal and that beneath my scepter a world of kings shall bow. The hot dark blood of that [a] black forefather—born king of men—is beating at my heart, and I know that I am either a genius or a fool. O I wonder what I am—I wonder what the world is—I wonder if life is worth the striving.[51]

Du Bois then announced the plans for the second quarter-century of his life: "These are my plans: to make a name in science, to make a name in literature and thus to raise my race. Or perhaps to raise a visible empire in Africa thro' England, France or Germany. I wonder what will be the outcome? Who knows?" In closing, Du Bois foreshadowed "Of the Coming of John" when he quoted Esther 4:16: "I will go unto the king—which is not according to the law and if I perish—I PER-ISH."[52]

This autobiographical dimension for "Of the Coming of John" is consistent with the argument that I make about John and gender inversion. The Book of Esther is a "coming out" story, though not necessarily a gay one. Esther is hiding the fact that she is a Jew, and she reveals her identity only when it is necessary to save her people, who have been slated for extermination. At the end of the book, when the Jews under the guidance of their queen stage a successful countergenocide against their enemies, they celebrate the Feast of Purim in her honor. Purim celebrants are encouraged to get drunk. As a part of this feast of excess, celebrants blur gender boundaries and cross-dress. Biblical scholar Timothy Beal explains the significance of this cross-dressing:

> Purim expresses its closeness to the text of Esther's play on the borderlines of self/other definition through its masquerades, and especially through masquerades that involve *transvesting*, that is, masquerades in which one crosses over a boundary line between identities that are culturally conceived as opposites. . . . It is not uncommon, for example, for contempo-

---

51. Lewis, *W. E. B. Du Bois—Biography of a Race*, 134.
52. Lewis, *W. E. B. Du Bois—Biography of a Race*, 135.

rary Purim plays to be done in drag, with women playing the male parts and men playing the female parts.[53]

Beal's concept of *transvesting* reinforces what I see as Du Bois's appropriation of the feminine for John. Beal states that when Esther "comes out" she "does not reveal her 'true' identity," rather she "revealed her *manyness*, her *excessiveness*—an 'I' with no single, integrating center, a locus of convergences that are often in tension with one another in ways that both put her in danger and carry potential for political subversion."[54] The "manyness and excessiveness" that Beal identifies in Esther would have been apparent to Du Bois, as his notebook entry reveals. Du Bois is a genius or possibly its antithesis, the fool. He both knows the world and is uncertain of it. His noble lineage recalls the trope of the "royal slave" that appeared in the writings of blacks throughout the eighteenth and nineteenth centuries.[55] Yet he is a slave who eventually shall subdue nations. His reference to the Book of Esther continues this multitude when he assumes simultaneously both male and female roles: the Persian King Ahasueras ("beneath my scepter a world of kings shall bow") and his supplicant queen, the Jewish Esther ("and if I perish, I perish").

The "manyness and excessiveness" in the Book of Esther even may be a source for Du Bois's concept of "double consciousness." Double consciousness, we remember, has no center and is in perpetual tension. Double consciousness, Du Bois writes, is produced in a world that yields the African American "no true self-consciousness," so he "ever feels his twoness,—an American, a Negro; two souls, two thoughts, two unreconciled strivings; two warring ideals in one dark body, whose dogged strength alone keeps it from being torn asunder."[56]

What we observe, then, in the story is another aspect of the Queen Esther motif. Du Bois's story is a narrative about concealment and hiding. Just as Esther hid her Jewish identity, John Jones has something to conceal, too. What Jones conceals is not that he is a homosexual man, since there is no evidence that John is even sexual, but by the end of the nineteenth century and the beginning of the heterosexual epoch, what Jones hides is "the closet of imagining *a* homosexual secret."[57] Lest we forget, John Jones has no erotic life. In queer theory,

---

53. Timothy Beal, *The Book of Hiding: Gender, Ethnicity, Annihilation, and Esther* (New York: Routledge, 1997), 123.
54. Beal, *Book of Hiding*, 123.
55. Barry Weller, "The Royal Slave and the Prestige of Origins," *Kenyon Review* 14, no. 3 (1992): 65–78.
56. Du Bois, *Souls*, 38.
57. Sedgwick, *Epistemology of the Closet*, 205.

the absence of the erotic life of a male character is in itself often taken as a sign of queerness. Not surprisingly, Du Bois refers to that which John hides as queer. When John leaves his home for college, he carries with him "a queer little trunk"; we never learn the contents of this trunk.[58] When John becomes serious about school and isolates himself from all others, he enters, Du Bois writes, "a queer thought world" where he entertains thoughts that "at times puzzled him sorely":

> He could not see just why the circle was not square, and carried it out fifty-six decimal places one midnight,—would have gone further, indeed, had not the matron rapped for lights out. He caught terrible colds lying on his back in the meadows of nights, trying to think out the solar system; he had grave doubts as to the ethics of the Fall of Rome, and strongly suspected the Germans of being thieves and rascals, despite his text-books; he pondered long over every new Greek word, and wondered why this meant that and why it couldn't mean something else, and how it must have felt to think all things in Greek. So he thought and puzzled along for himself,—pausing perplexed where the rest topped and surrendered.[59]

John's "queer thought world" corresponds to the modernist definition of queerness as something "strange, odd, peculiar, eccentric; suspicious, dubious; not in a normal condition, out of sorts; bad, worthless."[60] Mainly, though, John conceals his desire for homosocial union with his double—which in the Harvard speech was the Teutonic Strong Man, now represented by white John Henderson.

More relevant to the argument I am making here, the allusion to Queen Esther establishes the dilemma that Du Bois's protagonist faces: John assumes the risk of becoming temporarily effeminized as Queen Esther. However, John risks permanent effeminization since a racist society permits no legitimate movement of women across racial lines. Killing John Henderson resolves that dilemma; in effect, it shores up John Jones's untested masculinity.

An Unreliable Narrator Explains Violence

My approach to the story is at odds with standard readings that assume that John Jones kills his white double in defense of his sister. My approach is even at odds with ironic readings, such as Keith Byerman's, that John acts "to protect his sis-

58. Du Bois, *Souls*, 173.
59. Du Bois, *Souls*, 175.
60. Herrmann, *Queering the Moderns*, 6.

ter's honor in the tradition of [white] Southern chivalry."[61] Yet a close reading of the text reveals that John's motive for killing his white double is not clearly in defense of his sister. When John hears "a frightened cry" and sees "his dark sister struggling in the arms of a tall and fair-haired man," John says "not a word, but seizing a fallen limb," he strikes Henderson "with all the pent-up hatred of his great black arm." While the object of John's "hatred" is his white double, the reason for his hatred is not specified as loving and defending the sister. Once he has killed Jennie's assailant, John neither expresses concern for the sister he has rescued nor offers her any help. Jennie is not even mentioned after John kills his white double. In fact, she literally vanishes from the text. In the place where one might expect concern for Jennie or at least her presence, one finds only a description of John Henderson's dead body, which lays "white and still . . . bathed in sunshine and blood" while John "dreamily" gazes at it.[62] The very absence of concern or the narrator's voice for his sister, and, moreover, the substitution of the white male's slain body for Jennie calls into question the accepted idea that John kills his double because of his love for his sister.

That Du Bois uses violence to resolve this dilemma is noteworthy. Western societies allow males to use violence to resolve challenges to their masculinity (or what Signithia Fordham has called "gender integrity").[63] Du Bois makes this use of violence patently clear in the assault on his "gender integrity" recalled in the first chapter of *Souls*. Du Bois recounts how he and a group of classmates decided to exchange visiting cards, but a girl, presumably white, refused his. Anne Herrmann makes the astute observation that while the white girl's rejection is read as racial, it also "implies exclusion from heteronormativity."[64] The customs and laws that support miscegenation not only regulate race, they also "queer" black males by proscribing their ability to participate fully in heterosexuality. This understanding of queerness complicates a race-only reading when Du Bois writes that the girl's rejection made him realize that he "was different from the others" and "shut out from their world by a vast veil."[65] Not only is Du Bois writing about race, he is also writing against a culture that turns him queer by excluding him from public heterosexuality. We should remember that it is not at all unusual

61. Keith Byerman, *Seizing the Word: History, Art, and Self in the Work of W. E. B. Du Bois* (Athens: University of Georgia Press, 1994), 32.

62. Du Bois, *Souls*, 183.

63. Signithia Fordham, *Blacked Out: Dilemmas of Race, Identity, and Success at Capital High* (Chicago: University of Chicago Press, 1996), 279.

64. Herrmann, *Queering the Moderns*, 117.

65. Du Bois, *Souls*, 38.

for men to use violence against other men for allegedly denying them this right. "Homosexual panic," a diagnosis dating from the early 1920s, has also become a defense in the U.S. legal system for male defendants who claim they need to use violence to repel a sexual advance from a gay man.[66] Not surprisingly, Du Bois made it patently clear that violence was an acceptable means for resolving this queerness and thereby restoring his "gender integrity" when he wrote that after experiencing the greeting card incident, the "sky was bluest when I could beat my mates at examination-time, or beat them at a foot-race, or even *beat their stringy heads*."[67]

The violence Du Bois describes has as a historical referent the literary genre Sedgwick calls the "paranoid Gothic," "the Romantic novels in which a male hero is in a close, usually murderous relation to another male figure, in some respects his 'double,' to whom he seems to be mentally transparent."[68] Sedgwick's use of psychoanalysis is particularly useful for understanding the operation of homophobia in this genre; she writes that "paranoia is the psychosis that makes graphic the mechanisms of homophobia."[69] Sedgwick is clear that she is not implying that authors or the overall cultural effects of the novels in her study were homophobic, merely "that through these novels a tradition of homophobic thematics was a force" in the development of a particular literary genre. More specifically, Sedgwick contends that homophobia presents itself through a "thematics of absence."[70] "Of the Coming of John," with its violence of one double toward another "to whom he seems to be mentally transparent," belongs to this paranoid Gothic tradition. Absence in the story articulates itself or is most acutely noticed in the complete lack of sexuality in the protagonist. John's lack of sexuality is, I contend, the primary marker of a male homosexual panic.

Sexual Anesthesia

John's lack of sexuality is perhaps the most noteworthy aspect of the story. It may easily go unremarked because John is a bachelor; yet nowhere in the entire narrative arc of the story—which includes John's adolescence and young adulthood—are explicit sexual impulses either voiced by John or described by the narrator in

---

66. Henry T. Chuang and Donald Addington, "Homosexual Panic: A Review of Its Concept," *Canadian Journal of Psychiatry* 33 (1988): 613–17.
67. Du Bois, *Souls*, 38 (emphasis added).
68. Sedgwick, *Epistemology of the Closet*, 186.
69. Sedgwick, *Between Men*, 91.
70. Sedgwick, *Epistemology of the Closet*, 200.

relation to him. Du Bois seems to encourage a view of John as asexual, even when he places his protagonist in a large urban city (New York City) that would have held many erotic possibilities for a young man. John's failure or refusal to look for sexual companionship sharply contrasts with the behavior of his double. Henderson emerges in the text as a character who is (hetero)sexually charged, following the scenes with his date at the opera house and his exercise of the seigneurial rights of a southern white male by raping Jennie. In contrast, John remains alone throughout the story.

John's utter lack of sexual desire reflects the unreliability of the narrator when it comes to describing interracial violence. Here, the narrator's position is understandable given the reign of terror that whites wielded over black America at the turn of the century. As a result of this climate of terror, Du Bois in the guise of the short story's narrator continually sought to pacify and appease white readers, especially as the text relates interracial violence. One notable case occurs in his humanization of John Henderson in the same paragraph that describes Jennie's rape: Henderson "was not a bad fellow,—just a little spoiled and self-indulgent, and as headstrong as his proud father." This narration becomes odious when Jennie tries to evade her assailant, and the narrator diminishes the meaning of the white man's aggression as a "wilful mood" that "had seized the young idler" which caused him to "half mischievously" chase the young girl into the woods."[71]

Another notable example of the narrator's unreliability occurs at the opera house, with the elevation of John Henderson's white female date to "lady." Twice the narrator bestows the title "lady" upon the date, and, significantly, she is the only character to receive such elevation. This entitling establishes the deference appropriate to an encounter between a black male and a white female character; thus, when John accidentally touches her arm, no white reader could suspect her of soliciting the attentions of a black man. Such an accusation might provoke the white violence that Ida Wells experienced in the preceding decade, when she wrote in her 1892 pamphlet *Southern Horrors: Lynch Law in All Its Phases*, "White men lynch the offending Afro-American, not because he is a despoiler of virtue, but because he succumbs to the smiles of white women."[72] Angry white men destroyed Wells's printing press and vowed to kill her should she ever return to Memphis. The narrator in "Of the Coming of John" makes it clear to white and

71. Du Bois, *Souls*, 182.
72. Ida B. Wells, "Southern Horrors: Lynch Law in All Its Phases," in *Southern Horrors and Other Writings: The Anti-Lynching Campaign of Ida B. Wells, 1892–1900*, ed. Jacqueline Jones Royster (1892; Boston: Bedford, 1997), 54.

male readers that this story neither questions the virtue of white women nor calls upon white men to defend their honor.

On whose side is this narrator? John Jones's killing of his white double is the ultimate act of masculinity, for he behaves exactly as a white southern man would have been expected to in defense of his sister's honor. As Hazel Carby has pointed out, when John kills his double, Du Bois in effect "consciously confronts and contradicts claims that white male aggression is met only by black male passivity," and even though this confrontation leads to death, John's "manner of dying can be a model of manhood for future generations."[73] Yet at the same time, John is an embodiment of Queen Esther. He smites the enemies of his people, just as Esther had prophesized "and if I perish, I perish." And John Jones does indeed perish.

This is the case for "Of the Coming of John," where at the end of the tragic story Du Bois records his reaction to the rigid policing of race and sexuality by synecdoche—Wagnerian mourning substitutes for the regulation of the male homosocial bonds that make patriarchal national unity impossible. Although John risks temporarily effeminizing himself when he assumes the position of Queen Esther, there is no payoff. Racism makes it impossible for John to participate in any of the entitlements of biracial male bonding. John desires union with his white double, but he cannot act on it. For John to consolidate his relationship with his white double, he would have to participate with the double in the transaction of a woman; in other words, to act upon an interracial heterosexual desire. To do so would invite lynching. At the same time, Du Bois forecloses the possibility that a black female character become the object of John's sexuality. In fact, there is no eligible black female character in the short story. Du Bois deprives John of any desires that can be spoken. In effect, Du Bois creates "a thematics of absence," specifically unspeakability, which has been the code for male homosexuality throughout Christian history.

Conclusion

The focus of this essay has been a representation of male homosexual panic in fiction. I conclude this discussion in the multigenre spirit of *The Souls of Black Folk* by drawing attention to a case of autobiographical panic involving Du Bois. When he was editor of *The Crisis* magazine, some twenty-five years after the publication of *Souls*, Du Bois discovered that his business manager Augustus Granville

73. Carby, *Race Men*, 25.

Dill had been arrested for a homosexual encounter in a public lavatory.[74] Du Bois promptly dismissed Dill, a forty-six-year-old bachelor who had dedicated sixteen years of service to Du Bois and who hid his homosexual identity so successfully that he "had no other life than *The Crisis* and its master." Du Bois indicated the intensity of his relationship with Dill in a letter of termination, where he stated that he had never "contemplated continuing my life work without you by my side."[75] Du Bois's prompt dismissal of Dill resembles a classic instance of a homosexual panic at his discovery that the intimate bond that he had shared for so many years with Dill could be tainted by homosexuality.

More than thirty years later, and four years after Dill's death in 1956, Du Bois reflected, self-reproachfully, on this termination in his autobiography. The admission is noteworthy because it shows that Du Bois was still under the influence of the coercive double bind that regulates the male homosocial relationships he had earlier represented in "Of the Coming of John." Du Bois's recollection of the relationship is charged with barely disguised erotic desire. He writes, "In the midst of my career there *burst on me* a new and undreamed of aspect of sex. . . . A young man, long my disciple and student, then my co-helper and successor to part of my work, was suddenly arrested for molesting men in public places" (emphasis added). Is Du Bois describing an orgasm or an assault when he writes "there burst on me"? Is Du Bois alluding to the classical Mediterranean institution of pederasty with its teacher-disciple relationship? Despite the erotic subtext, Du Bois claims ignorance when he writes that he had "no conception of homosexuality" and had "never understood the tragedy of an Oscar Wilde."[76] Nevertheless, homosexuality repulses Du Bois, and he intuitively knows that his actions have to be swift and irrevocable. So, Du Bois writes, "I dismissed my co-worker forthwith, and spent heavy days regretting my act."[77] Du Bois was attracted to Dill, but the young man's homosexuality was a betrayal of that attraction. What is startling about Du Bois's admission is its unreliability. Du Bois says that he regrets an "act," and a reader might prematurely assume that the referent is Du Bois's recognition of the perniciousness of homophobia. However, the "act" that

74. For the most complete biographical sketch of Dill's life, see Theodore Kornwiebel, "Augustus Granville Dill," in *Dictionary of American Negro Biography*, ed. Rayford W. Logan and Michael R. Winston (New York: Norton, 1982), 177–78.

75. David Levering Lewis, *W. E. B. Du Bois—The Fight for Equality and the American Century, 1919–1963* (New York: Holt, 2000), 205.

76. W. E. B. Du Bois, *The Autobiography of W. E. B. Du Bois: A Soliloquy on Viewing My Life from the Last Decade of Its First Century* (New York: International Publishers, 1968), 282.

77. Du Bois, *The Autobiography*, 282.

Du Bois regrets is unclear and therefore not easily named, and it parallels the epistemological uncertainties in "Of the Coming of John." Is Du Bois lamenting having dismissed Dill for his homosexuality? Is he lamenting that Dill was a homosexual? Or was Du Bois attracted to Dill, and is he now faced with the fear of having that attraction?

In any event, the queering "I do" of Du Bois's short story is historically bound. The homosocial continuum through which men gained entitlement speaks of ambiguity, fluidity, and a lack of fixity. Without rigid policing the homosocial can become homosexual, as Du Bois feared with respect to his relationship with Dill. Miscegenation was another form of policing the boundaries of male homosociality that excluded black men from a place of equality with white men. Du Bois records his recognition of this policing as a trauma in *The Souls of Black Folk*, first in the greeting card incident of its first chapter and in what was initially to be the closing chapter, "Of the Coming of John." One might begin to question the degree to which the final chapter, "The Sorrow Songs," is an attempt to conceal Du Bois's panic.

This essay's historical foundation lies in the fact that Du Bois was part of an intellectual group that was creating sexual identity categories. Du Bois uses the scene of Wagnerian mourning to lament the impossible compact of white and black men in late-nineteenth-century America. The failure of biracial unity is referenced through a story of gender inversion, sexual panic, and violence. Sedgwick writes that there is little reason "why . . . 'male homosexual panic' could not just as descriptively have been called 'male heterosexual panic'—or, simply, 'male sexual panic.' "[78] Du Bois's melodramatic ending of this short story is a recording of homosexual panic or an apprehension of his inability to participate in socially accepted public heterosexuality. Black John Jones must kill his beloved, white John Henderson, if he is to restore his own gender integrity. This panic or apprehension can only end in the death of queer desire within the confines of the bourgeois morality that exists in "Of the Coming of John."

Charles I. Nero teaches at Bates College in the Department of Rhetoric and the Programs in African American Studies and American Cultural Studies. His most recent works appear in vol. 56 of *Camera Obscura* (2004) and in *Black Queer Studies in the Millennium* (forthcoming).

78. Sedgwick, *Epistemology of the Closet*, 200.

Du Bois and the Production of the Racial Picturesque

Sheila Lloyd

*It is true that an observer, under that softening influence of the fine
arts which makes other people's hardships picturesque, might have
been delighted with this homestead called Freeman's End. . . . So called
apparently by way of sarcasm, to imply that a man was free to quit it
if he chose, but that there was no earthly "beyond" open to him.*
George Eliot, *Middlemarch*

With her characteristic understatement, George Eliot exposes the English bourgeoisie's use of picturesque art to affirm its self-identification and selectively to ignore aspects of reality. However, where Eliot questions the bourgeoisie's assertion of its own interests at the expense of the laboring classes, W. E. B. Du Bois, in *The Souls of Black Folk*,[1] questions the racial self-identification and interests of white America—which he takes on as social and metatheoretical problems. Thus, rather than dismissing the picturesque as Eliot does, Du Bois finds that it can be recoded so that it functions instead to promote social critique, foster sociability across racial lines, and transform self-interest into an interest in others. All of this might explain why, in several key moments of *Souls*, Du

I thank Donna Landry, Kathryne Lindberg, Ted Pearson, and the *Public Culture* anonymous reader for providing me with valuable insights and editorial suggestions. The first three, I hope, know how grateful I am to have received their constant support of my work.

1. W. E. B. Du Bois, *The Souls of Black Folk*, in *Writings* (New York: Literary Classics of the United States/Viking, 1986). Hereafter referred to as *Souls*.

Public Culture 17(2): 277–97

Bois appropriates language associated with the picturesque aesthetic and produces what I am referring to as a "racial picturesque," in which a language of social analysis and critique is supplemented by romantic vocabulary and imagery. By aestheticizing the social and political landscape of early-twentieth-century America, Du Bois takes the risky step of creating a textual environment that, while not directly reflecting a real social environment, invites a coming to terms with the notion that the racial picturesque can reveal important aspects of the Negro problem and of our ways of approaching it.

The racial picturesque engenders a mobile subject who is sensitive to racial and other social inequalities. Facilitating the process of transforming a presumed knowledge into interests, Du Bois constructs a textual environment from the diverse tropes of the picturesque, specifically those remarking vistas, vantages, prospects, and other objects comprehended in spatial terms. By means of the picturesque, Du Bois's narrator shows a different face of the land and challenges the reader (about whom more will be said) to see and to respond differently to the signifiers representing the Negro problem. As writer rather than as narrator, Du Bois has two tasks: to motivate the reader to comprehend the color line and its effects on whites as well as blacks and to supplement conventional formulations from sociology and political economy with aesthetics, their seemingly polar opposite.[2]

Like Du Bois's fictive reader, readers today are asked to engage the metatheoretical questions upon which he works. Such questions appear in Du Bois's early writings, and there is continuity in the line of thought that produced "The Study of the Negro Problem," delivered in 1897 before the American Academy of Political and Social Science, and his proposal six years later in *Souls* that the "Negro problem," the problem of the color line, will become the "problem of problems" for the twentieth century. In his earlier address, Du Bois clearly states the methodological difficulties of extant investigations of the Negro problem, and he is acutely aware that scholarly concerns are not irrelevant when compared to the bare facts of oppression. He also indicates that what might be deemed the merely cultural or rhetorical are significant ways by which we begin to understand, take a position on, and attempt to resolve social problems. As he puts it, "However difficult it may be to know all about the Negro, it is certain that we can know vastly more than we do."[3] The racial picturesque is one of the ways in which we can know, and perhaps do, more.

2. Ross Posnock argues for the compatibility of aesthetic and political discourses in Du Bois's writings and encourages those who would insist that they are incompatible to recall a similar articulation in "Western Marxism," particularly the Frankfurt school. See Posnock, "The Distinction of Du Bois: Aesthetics, Pragmatism, Politics," *American Literary History* 7 (1995): 500–524.

3. W. E. B. Du Bois, "The Study of the Negro Problem," in *The Seventh Son: The Thought and Writings of W. E. B. Du Bois*, vol. 1, ed. Julius Lester (New York: Vintage, 1971), 236.

The Scene and Vision of the Negro Problem

As a mode of representation, the picturesque is concerned with vision, which makes it an interesting subject for the problematic of identification, one of Du Bois's metatheoretical concerns. At the same time that the picturesque appears to make what it gazes upon clear and to unify it conceptually, it also finesses the fact that it can do neither. With this, Du Bois as narrator inaugurates his relationship with his "Gentle Reader," who, from the beginning, he wants to make aware of the fantasy of potency informing the reader's preconceptions about the text. Moreover, he wants that reader to notice his own limited horizon and to identify with an-other place—not the actual scene of the reader's everyday life, but one that the reader comes to invest with an affirmative character. This "other" place can only be seen upon coming behind the Veil. In this sense, the picturesque scene that Du Bois creates by placing the reader in a particular line of vision causes him to anticipate that there is something more beyond what he believes he is seeing, and this something more is the Veil itself.[4]

In effect, Du Bois is asking the reader to imagine himself as a picturesque traveler who, from within the Veil and on the other side of the color line, experiences the space of the nation in a way that involves interrogating many of the official attributes constituting the "National Symbolic."[5] In acquainting his reader with an unofficial narrative concerning national deformation and reconstitution, he establishes that the task of reading defamiliarizes much of what the reader has assumed about his nation and its history. He posits his reader as a citizen-traveler with whom he shares an identification that, in the first chapter, requires the reader to ask the unasked question he has all along wanted to pose to his racialized

4. I use the masculine not as a generic, but to specify the subject of the racial picturesque produced in *Souls*. Quite frequently, Du Bois uses masculine pronouns and/or envisions the remaking of the social world as a task undertaken by men. Some examples can be found on 359, 435–36, 436, 440–41, 490, and 519 of the text.

5. This term comes from Lauren Berlant, who explains that "we are bound together because we inhabit the political space of the nation, which is not merely juridical, territorial (*jus soli*), genetic (*jus sanguinis*), linguistic, or experiential, but some tangled cluster of these. I call this space the 'National Symbolic.' Law dominates the field of citizenship, constructing technical definitions of the citizen's rights, duties, and obligations. But the National Symbolic also aims to link regulation to desire, harnessing affect to political life through the production of 'national fantasy.' By 'fantasy' I mean to designate how national culture becomes local—through the images, narratives, monuments, and sites that circulate through personal/collective consciousness." Berlant, *The Anatomy of National Fantasy: Hawthorne, Utopia, and Everyday Life* (Chicago: University of Chicago Press, 1991), 4–5. The picturesque, as I conceive of it here, can be thought of as part and parcel of the National Symbolic that Berlant describes.

other[6] and urges the other to venture some word once the question has been posed. Du Bois suggests: "Between me and the other world there is ever an unasked question: unasked by some through feelings of delicacy, by others through the difficulty of framing it. All, nevertheless, flutter round it. They approach me in a half-hesitant sort of way, eye me curiously or compassionately, . . . instead of saying directly, How does it feel to be a problem? . . . To the real question, How does it feel to be a problem? I answer seldom a word."[7]

The deadlock here suggests that something intrinsic to this problem makes it resist symbolization. In this founding rhetorical situation, the compassion, curiosity, and reticence that the onlookers share reflect a preexisting structure of feeling that Du Bois takes advantage of when providing a frame for posing and answering their question. What is interesting about the constructed frame is that it turns on a highly subjectivized language to explain the meanings of the color line. There are two aspects to his textual resolution of this initial deadlock: an identification between narrator and reader and the creation of a social code adequate for representing the Negro.

After expressing the difficulties involved in a discussion with those who do not see how the Negro problem pertains to them, Du Bois begins that fraught dialogue not in a social key, but in one that personalizes for himself and for his reader the experience of feeling that one is a problem. In his initial exploration of his first strange experience of this feeling, he implicitly borrows from language that we might readily associate with literary pictorialism, language used to "draw" a scene: "It is in the early days of rollicking boyhood that the revelation first bursts upon one, all in a day, as it were. I remember well when the shadow swept across me. I was a little thing, away up in the hills of New England, where the dark Housatonic winds between Hoosac and Taghkanic to the sea. In a wee schoolhouse, something put it into the boys' and girls' heads to buy gorgeous visiting-cards—ten cents a package—and exchange."[8] This scene of racial revelation, of what will be the subject's entrance into a racialized symbolic, solicits identification from the reader—a northern, educated, white man who, if not familiar with the specific landscape or scene that the narrator describes, is aware of the

6. In keeping with Lacan's distinction between the small "other" and the big "Other," my phrase "racialized other" designates a subject that is both different from the self and a part of the self. This relationship is captured in Lacan's neologism "extimacy." The big Other acts within the symbolic through law and language; I refer to this sense in the following sections, where I describe "the southern symbolic system."

7. Du Bois, *Souls*, 363.

8. Du Bois, *Souls*, 363–64.

place of this New England terrain in the National Symbolic. The hermeneutic resulting from the reader's tendentiously subjective absorption in the text allows the narrator to redraw the map of the North that the reader may have already produced cognitively. The new map defamiliarizes the old and delineates a scene in which a proferred object, circulating within an economy commodifying intimate relations, is rejected by someone new to the idyllic natural scene and community that Du Bois describes. What emerges in this portrait of the children's imitation of adults is something that manifests one of the social order's inconsistencies, an inconsistency unknown to the young Du Bois. The insight here establishes the overlap of imaginary misrecognition and symbolic circulation.

The narrative transition from the natural to the social world and from the social to the subjective (or the autobiographical, whereby Du Bois's experiences become exemplary) brings the narrator and the white male citizen-reader together for the common purpose of breaking their initial deadlock. Structurally, what helps Du Bois move them beyond their stalled discursive position is the creation of a triangular relationship whereby his new classmate, a white girl who refuses the visiting card, occupies one of the axes along which the letter moves. Along the other two axes are Du Bois and his white male reader. What the young girl's refusal sets in motion—and this is why she is structurally necessary in the exchange that ensues between narrator and reader—is not only the return of the letter to Du Bois but his recirculation of it, thus ensuring, to paraphrase Lacan, that the letter does indeed arrive at its destination. The circulation, far more than the letter itself, establishes the narrator's symbolic destiny or the position that he occupies as one newly made a subject by racialization.

By placing his white male reader simultaneously inside and outside the system presented in the anecdote, Du Bois grants him the "innocence" that precedes the revelation of there being a problem. Having the citizen-reader witness the socially symbolic interaction that occurs along the other two axes permits Du Bois to imply that sight aids in the creation of the meaningful bond he wants to establish with his reader. In other words, by injuring his reader's innocence, he wants to change not only what the reader sees but how he sees. The circulation of the letter among the narrator, the schoolgirl, and the reader frames that "letter" as the Negro problem—which, in the anecdote, Du Bois does not recognize himself as representing, the girl shrinks from, and the reader misrecognizes as having made him, as much as Du Bois, what he is.

Since so much in the first chapter's opening paragraphs, and arguably in the text as a whole, depends on where one stands, we need not belabor this point. However, it is worth remarking that Du Bois exploits the picturesque doubling of vision (i.e., what is seen and what lies beyond what is seen) in order to approach the problem of the color line via a form that aestheticizes, envisions, and narrativizes the problem's workings and thereby reveals its contingency. Consider how the movements of the two rivers coursing through the Berkshire valley of his childhood are so much like the mobility that he projects psychically and aesthetically (as well as socially and historically) throughout the text. Thus in the unfolding drama that is the souls of black folk, Du Bois invests his language with marks of psychic and aesthetic contingency and thereby explores the distance between social reality and its representation.

The signature figure for this distance is the Veil, a paradoxical troping revealing the manner in which one looks at oneself from the point of view of the Other. The problem with using this figure to gauge the distance between social reality and its representation lies in the incommensurability between its rhetorical efficacy and its perceptual indeterminacy; that is, the alternation of concealment and revelation constitutive of the Veil. This said, the Veil's critical and hermeneutical functions of discernment and imaginative comprehension rely on preestablished, yet malleable, cultural and political identities, with which Du Bois frames and perspectivizes the scenes he points out throughout the textual journey within the Veil. Laying this field open as an entire surface of discourses, practices, institutions, and disciplines, he motivates his reader to develop a sensibility or an affect that is responsive to his recurrent use of the visual language of the picturesque.[9] Given, however, the deadlock between self and other, his initial reader-text model (established by the circulation of the letter) seems ill-suited for taking the measure of reality and its representation. Instead, a model showing the relation between social movement and cultural formation—that is, the Veil as border or frontier—appears more capable of breaking the conceptual deadlock of the symbolic and social rather than the abstract, and mistakenly real, significance of being black.

The potential for social movement within the Veil depends on what occurs in the process of such movement. Du Bois pursues this point by imaginatively recasting the narrator and reader, whom we saw in the first chapter, as companions who in chapter 7, "Of the Black Belt," travel through Georgia. Their movement suggests a "transient presence . . . in the [textual] landscape" of the Veil, and this presence leads to sensational impressions.[10] These impressions, moreover,

9. See Thomas Pfau, *Wordsworth's Profession: Form, Class, and the Logic of Early Romantic Cultural Production* (Stanford, Calif.: Stanford University Press, 1997), 11.

10. Kim Michasiw, "Nine Revisionist Theses on the Picturesque," *Representations* 38 (1992): 82. I thank my colleague Robert Aguirre for bringing this essay to my attention.

potentially become material for the traveler's increased capacity to connect what lies before him to what he already "knows" ideologically. By means of seeing and appreciating the landscape and by means of storing up memories about the people and things in that space, the traveler assimilates the known with the unknown. This much was the impetus behind the Grand Tour, by which young men from England spent time on the Continent improving and expanding their knowledge.[11] But whereas the power-knowledge relation emerging from the Grand Tour is invested in mastery and sovereignty that offer the subject a premature sense of accomplishment, the epistemic and social returns for Du Bois's citizen-reader-traveler are less easy to discern. Like those gentlemen-scholars who converted leisurely travel into a mode of learning and being, Du Bois's citizen-reader-traveler might come to believe that traversing the Black Belt (especially with Du Bois, the narrator, as guide) would result in his mastering all aspects of the Negro problem. Traveling in the company of someone he believes will tell him the "truth," the reader willingly suspends certain conventions and inconveniences himself. Yet looking at and comprehending (i.e., studying) the Negro problem cannot be an exercise in mastery, and it cannot yield any unqualified verities. Instead, all that can be guaranteed is an encounter between the subject and the ideological remainder that is part of the social interests of his time. This remainder involves psychopolitical techniques that pass themselves off as small and insignificant responses to particular social and cultural demands.

The Racial Picturesque in the Age of Sensibility: Du Bois on Sympathy and Cooperation

By examining Du Bois's solicitation of affective and critical responses from the reader and his rhetorical strategy for provoking an introjective identification, we note how Du Bois establishes a pattern in the text of shuttling between social and aesthetic discourses for the purpose of overcoming the alienation between whites and blacks. In a telling instance of this, he writes, "In a world where it means so much to take a man by the hand and sit beside him, to look frankly into his eyes

11. After the Napoleonic wars, travel to the Continent became possible, and young men finished their educations by studying and traveling there. During their visits, many of them encountered the works of artists, such as Claude Loraine, known for their picturesque landscapes. The Grand Tour itself was informed by searching for and retracing paths deemed picturesque. The ideology of the picturesque for these travelers and for those who offered instruction in the creation of picturesque images was one of the ways by which the English bourgeoisie began to represent itself culturally as a distinctive class. Pfau deals with this extensively in the first two chapters of *Wordsworth's Profession*.

and feel his heart beating red with blood; in a world where a social cigar or a cup of tea together means more than legislative halls and magazine articles and speeches,—one can imagine the consequences of the almost utter absence of such social amenities between estranged races."[12] Here and elsewhere in chapter 9, "Of the Sons of Master and Man," we find that the means of political agitation that Du Bois had favored thus far in his career lack something when placed alongside this sociability across the color line. Considering his claims on the efficacy of hands, hearts, and eyes in transforming extant relations between the "better" blacks and whites, we might expect the diction and tone of his portrayal of these racial and affective representatives to be consistent with these claims. What we find, however, is that this portrayal is embedded in a language of social critique.

For Du Bois, sympathy is a figure of repetition and—like his retrieval and redeployment of the figurative language of the picturesque—functions to question the silencing of words. Likewise, his use of anaphoric phrasing joins with his argument regarding interracial sociability and allows him to insist that "in a land where the tyranny of public opinion and the intolerance of criticism is for obvious historical reasons so strong as in the South, such a situation is extremely difficult to correct . . . many a scheme of friendliness and philanthropy, of broad-minded sympathy and generous fellowship between the two [races] has dropped still-born because some busybody has forced the color-question to the front and brought the tremendous force of unwritten law against the innovators."[13] These small details of social relations appear to us as "the humble but concrete form of every morality," which since the eighteenth century had been at the foundation of antislavery and antiracist thought and politics.[14]

Yet while we might be inclined to acknowledge this antiracist and antislavery politics *as* politics, we also have to read them as psychopolitical techniques (and, in my opinion, failing at this renders us unable to question what these techniques, as morality and charity, were meant to change). The importance of incorporating these elements in our analysis of the Negro problem becomes obvious when we find ourselves forced to ask what Du Bois is getting at when he states, "In regard to the social contact between the races, . . . nothing has come to replace that finer sympathy and love between some masters and house servants which the radical and more uncompromising drawing of the color-line in recent years has caused

12. Du Bois, *Souls*, 409.
13. Du Bois, *Souls*, 489.
14. Quotation is from Michel Foucault, *Discipline and Punish: The Birth of the Prison*, trans. Alan Sheridan (New York: Vintage, 1995), 223.

almost completely to disappear."[15] Are we to compare the transaction between writer and reader to the finer sympathy for which he demonstrates nostalgia? Or are we to consider that the interaction between the social situations of literary production and literary reception promotes a sensibility that accords to desire, affect, and the aesthetic a place in the political project of querying and dismantling the color line, a project that will mean settling the debts accumulated by racial antagonism and oppression?

To clarify this, we have to re-pose the question of why desire and affect, as well as the aesthetic notions related to the picturesque, are such important features of *Souls*. That it allows us to do this is yet another example of how the text, in its linguistic as well as its thematic guise, expresses a social critique that broaches the limits of racial sympathy and cooperation and conjoins those with some of the limits of the social. Considered along these lines, the yoking of the aesthetic with affect and an understanding of both as social in nature are not incomprehensible. *Souls* historicizes sympathy as a complicated social and political tactic by means of which those who self-consciously adopt the position of "feeling with others" can consider this not an individual act but one that publicizes social and ethical responses. This argument on sympathy appears most explicitly in chapter 12, "Of Alexander Crummell."

In his historical account of the uses to which sympathy has been put, Du Bois writes:

> The nineteenth was the first century of human sympathy,—the age when half wonderingly we began to descry in others that transfigured spark of divinity which we call Myself; when clodhoppers and peasants, and tramps and thieves, and millionaires and—sometimes—Negroes, became throbbing souls whose warm pulsing life touched us so nearly that we half gasped with surprise, crying "Thou too! Hast Thou seen Sorrow and the dull waters of Hopelessness? Hast Thou known Life?" And then all helplessly we peered into those Other-worlds, and wailed, "O World of Worlds, how shall man make you one?"[16]

This refers generally to sympathy in nineteenth-century America where, as in England, it conjoined ideology and aesthetics. Among the proponents of this with respect to the picturesque was John Ruskin, who, in his diary entry for May 11, 1854, recalls a scene along the Somme River in Amiens:

15. Du Bois, *Souls*, 489.
16. Du Bois, *Souls*, 514.

All exquisitely picturesque, and as miserable as picturesque. We delight in seeing the figures in boats pushing them about the bits of water in Prout's drawings, but as I look to-day at the unhealthy face and melancholy, apathetic mien of the man in the boat, pushing his load of peat along the ditch, and of the people, men and women, who sat spinning gloomily in the picturesque cottages, I could not help feeling how many suffering persons must pay for my picturesque subject, and my happy walk.[17]

What becomes apparent in juxtaposing Du Bois's and Ruskin's statements is Du Bois's reclamation of Ruskin's ethical version of the picturesque, whether narrative or visual, as an intimate response to both natural and social environments.

Ethically and ideologically, Du Bois takes a language of abstraction and uses it to concretize the socially determinant figures of peasants, thieves, and even Negroes. He does this in three ways. First, the action and consequences of unveiling are arrived at by means of the narrated event of "descrying in others . . . Myself." Secondly, while seemingly suggestive of a narcissistic regard, this metaphor of revelation stands for interaction and conflict between individuals: it is suggested that "we" who "half gasped with surprise" cannot serve as the subject of the enunciated or narrated statement, nor as the enunciating subject of that "half gasped" cry, without seeing a relationship between negotiation and conflict, a relationship which is linguistic and social. In other words, the narrated event indicates that sympathy results in the ability to sense and to begin to understand new details in the world. The speech event or utterance of the discovery of sympathy makes ironic the coincidence of sympathy and antipathy in the same social space and in actual individuals. Finally, what at the end of the passage appears as a "mere" psychic and affective reaction—"all helplessly we peered into those Other-worlds, and wailed, 'O World of Worlds, how shall man make you one?'"—is in fact the social cause of what is narrated: namely, the refusal to accord social recognition to others. We might take this reading of the progress of human sympathy and see it as opening a moral domain. However, in my preferred reading of the passage, which does not pretend to cancel a "moral" one, the passage's status as a speech-event or an utterance is to be understood in social and, indeed, in political terms.[18]

This logic is repeated in Du Bois's address to a figure he calls the "armchair

17. John Ruskin, *The Diaries of John Ruskin, 1848–1873*, ed. Joan Evans and John Howard Whitehouse (Oxford, U.K.: Clarendon, 1958), 493.

18. For more on these distinctions, see John Brenkman, *Culture and Domination* (Ithaca, N.Y.: Cornell University Press, 1987), 115–16. I am indebted to Brenkman in the reading I present here.

sociologist." To the seeker of knowledge who depends solely on and trusts statistics, who is unwilling to immerse himself in the actual lives they represent, he
states, "I have thus far sought to make clear the physical, economic, and political
relations of the Negroes and whites in the South as I have conceived them. . . . But
after all that has been said on these more tangible matters of human contact, there
still remains a part essential to a proper description of the South which it is difficult to describe in terms easily understood by strangers."[19] Here, then, is another
deadlock—one that results not from the difficulty of explaining "how it feels to be
a problem," but rather from that of doing so in light of the social relations along
the color line. Thus, at the very moment in "Of the Sons of Master and Man" that
Du Bois presents his argument on sympathy and cooperation, he seems to depart
from a primarily sociological language because he finds "a part essential" to his
argument that eludes that discursive register. Having done its work of accounting
for and explaining those matters that pertain to the "study of the companion-
able man," sociology appears unable to address the elusive "part essential" that
remains. And the prominence of this remainder in the passage cited recalls the
interlocutory deadlock that obtained between those within and those without the
Veil. In each situation, something cannot be properly accounted for or properly
expressed. What may be less obvious is that, in spite of his intimations, this difficulty must be seen as a problem for Du Bois and not solely for strangers (i.e.,
northerners, of whom Du Bois is one) or for those outside the Veil (who occupy
a social position determined and designated as white). Although he has ignored
this problem as it pertains to his own situation—as much as to that of his white
northern reader qua potential interpreter of the South—we find him sufficiently
aware of it to cast about for some way to depict that "part essential to a proper
description of the South" and "the Negro problem." The discursive and political
problems are coextensive.

This is suggested in a passage redolent of the imagery and language of literary
romanticism, the entirety of which bears citing:

> It is in fine, the atmosphere of the land, the thought and feeling, the thou-
> sand and one little actions which go to make up life. In any community or
> nation it is these little things which are most elusive to grasp and yet most
> essential to any clear conception of the group life taken as a whole. What
> is thus true of all communities is peculiarly true of the South, where, out-
> side of written history and outside of printed law, there has been going on
> for a generation as deep a storm and stress of human souls, as intense a

19. Du Bois, *Souls*, 487.

ferment of feeling, as intricate a writhing of spirit, as ever a people experienced. Within and without the somber veil of color vast social forces have been at work,—efforts for human betterment, movements toward disintegration and despair, tragedies and comedies in social and economic life, and a swaying and lifting and sinking of human hearts which have made this land a land of mingled sorrow and joy, of change and excitement and unrest.[20]

The passage's diction endeavors to capture that elusive element, or remainder, "after all has been said on [the] more tangible matters of human contact." And as noted earlier, the difficulty of apprehending this is not only a problem for the so-called stranger, but also for Du Bois as writer and analyst. A potential discursive solution to the difficulties posed by something that resists symbolization is produced in a picturesque language concerning "the atmosphere of the land." After acknowledging the inability of the disciplinary language of sociology to provide a fully "clear conception of the group life taken as a whole," Du Bois turns to the language that had, for more than a century, been most frequently associated with the picturesque.

This other language mediates the relations he attempts to create between writer and reader by placing them in a common position. However, insofar as this position reveals analytic and discursive limitations *and* shared sensibilities, it does not a singular perspective make, especially since Du Bois presents himself as controlling the discursive environment he creates by using the picturesque. What is significant nonetheless is that the copositioning of writer and reader belies a responsiveness to cultural and linguistic idioms that do not draw exclusively on sociological terms. In other words, the limits of the sociological mode make possible the reemergence of another mode of response and representation. Moreover, the reciprocal identification between the personae of the author and the reader is assumed to rely on these discursive relationships. Well aware of the history concerning the social construction of these personae and of the literary convention wherein the persona called the writer finds common ground with that called the reader, Du Bois enjoins his reader to become literate in the thematic and cultural notions and forms at his disposal. Much of this has implications for the reader's comprehension that the Negro problem is his problem, too.[21]

To convey this, Du Bois relies on the cultural and class assumption that his

20. Du Bois, *Souls*, 487–88.
21. Compare a similar claim made by Lewis Gordon in *Existentia Africana: Understanding Africana Existential Thought* (New York: Routledge, 2000), 62–95.

reader is aware of the late eighteenth- and early nineteenth-century literature of Sturm und Drang, and he trusts his reader's ability to recognize such borrowings in characterizations of the South as a place "where outside of written history and outside of printed law, there has been going on for a generation as deep *a storm and stress of human souls*, as intense *a ferment of feeling*, as intricate *a writhing of spirit*, as ever a people experience."[22] Attempting to devise ways to represent the properties of "group life" adequately, Du Bois does two things: he borrows from the language of German and English romanticisms, and he employs that language to represent the otherwise unreportable properties of a people's experience in order to demonstrate that, despite their immateriality, they are sometimes "materialized in certain features."[23] This accords with my reading of the resistances to symbolization that Du Bois encounters initially when trying to explain the color line and the Negro problem.

In this instance, what does not explicitly manifest itself in the symbolic system of the social order cannot be understood as nonexistent, which apparently is what he advances when referring to an "outside of written history and outside of printed law." What exceed written history and printed law are actually the unwritten and implicit rules that institute and regulate modes of social interaction within the symbolic system of the South. Unwritten, unseen, unspeakable, but not unsymbolizable, these rules are actualized both in social practices and affective responses. The psychopolitical techniques, of which these practices and responses are a modality, work upon the subject and perhaps prove to be more effective in enforcing their mandates. Despite his interest in the South and his increasing sympathy for those whom he sees as himself, the citizen-reader in *Souls* seems surprised by these shadowy manifestations of unwritten laws. Perhaps he does not recognize that he has been unsettled and recomposed by the hand of those laws determining what is socially acceptable and mandating his symbolic place. All of this leads to the question: why is it necessary for the citizen-reader to see himself not seeing?

As with Du Bois's armchair sociologist who has been inclined to look very narrowly at what arrests his attention, something similar is involved for

> the casual observer visiting the South [who] sees at first little of [the freed-men's sons' struggle]. He notes the growing frequency of dark faces as he rides along, . . . and this little world seems as happy and contented as other

22. Du Bois, *Souls*, 487 (emphasis added).
23. Renata Salecl presents this formulation in her introduction to *Sexuation*, ed. Renata Salecl (Durham, N.C.: Duke University Press, 2000), 4–5.

worlds he has visited. Indeed, on the question of questions—the Negro problem—he hears so little that there almost seems to be a conspiracy of silence; the morning papers seldom mention it, and then usually in a far-fetched academic way, and indeed almost every one seems to forget and ignore the darker half of the land, until the astonished visitor is inclined to ask if after all there is any problem here.[24]

Here, Du Bois insists that his reader notice the armchair sociologist's and the casual observer's failures of vision. But why does he press this demand on his reader? In part, he has his reader consider how, in order for the sociologist and casual observer to remark what they do seem to register, they have to leave something unobserved, which would seem inevitable given the fact that one cannot see everything and must make discriminations. Yet even with this awareness, Du Bois's two figures seem disappointed not to see and hear more. The personal nature of the expert's and the dilettante's frustrated desires appears to be similar, and to some extent they are. However, the difference is that the casual observer may be the better placed to take a second look and to open himself to sensations—physical and affective—that the expert believes he cannot risk indulging for the sake of professional disinterestedness. In the end, this might explain why Du Bois's reader minimally has to understand the shortcomings of being a short-sighted and unsympathetic subject divested of any stake or interest in what he attempts to see.

Intimacy and Imagination: Affective Mediations of the Social

In the reading of *Souls* I have been developing, intimacy and affect are doubly configured as the recomposition of a social environment and as the composition of a textual one. Although, as the epigraph from Eliot indicates, the classical picturesque resists the interpenetration of the social and the textual or pictorial, *Souls* juxtaposes them. One effect of this contiguity is to open up the text to other thoughts on composition—including the conflation of literary romanticism with the picturesque creation of personal meaning, the images that render history palpable, and the possibility of developing a critical hermeneutic on intimacy. Three moments suffice to demonstrate this. The relation between the first two appears in "Of the Black Belt." The third interprets cultural forms comprising intimacy and affect.

Imaginatively figured and rhetorically structured as what Robert Stepto has

---

24. Du Bois, *Souls*, 488.

called a "journey of immersion," "Of the Black Belt" addresses movement, containment, distance, and proximity.[25] The cognitive and historical maps consulted throughout the symbolically picturesque journey through Georgia, which Du Bois claims is "the geographical focus of our Negro population," make historical recollection an act of gathering impressions and images.[26] These become useful for the exploitation of the field of fantasy that is the National Symbolic. Showing what is involved in inhabiting that field, Du Bois calls his citizen-traveler-reader's attention to

> the crimson soil of Georgia stretching away bare and monotonous. . . . Here and there lay straggling, unlovely villages, and lean men loafed leisurely at the depots; then again came the stretch of pines and clay. . . . This is historic ground. Right across our track, three hundred and sixty years ago, wandered the cavalcade of Hernando de Soto. . . . Here sits Atlanta, the city of a hundred hills, with something Western, something Southern, and something quite its own, in its busy life. And a little past Atlanta, to the southwest is the land of the Cherokees, and there, not far from where Sam Hose was crucified, you may stand on a spot which is to-day the centre of the Negro problem—the centre of those nine million who are America's dark heritage from slavery and the slave-trade.[27]

The deictic movement and organization of this passage reflect the travelers' movement across "historic ground," where the landscape and people outside the window of the train signify less to them than does the imaginatively and textually composed landscape of the mind. Or so it would seem. In fact, the actual and the imagined landscape are continuous, which leads Du Bois to question the presumed distance between social reality and its representation by aesthetic means. Although he and his companion move quickly past the spots marked as being of historical significance, Du Bois as narrator does not fail to mention the current condition of the actual landscape.

Quite obviously, the image presented is one that is generically picturesque, but the framing phrases—"monotonous," "straggling," "unlovely," and "lean" at the beginning of the account and "America's dark heritage from slavery and the slave-trade" at the end—create the impression of a return to a social space whose features have been shaped and determined by specific means—thereby Du Bois

25. See Robert B. Stepto, *From behind the Veil: A Study of Afro-American Narrative* (Urbana: University of Illinois Press, 1979), 66–82.
26. Du Bois, *Souls*, 440.
27. Du Bois, Souls, 439–40.

recomposes a generic picturesque into a racial picturesque. The unpleasing sights just beyond the travelers have economic, political, and social antecedents, among which slavery and the slave trade are only two, and it is these that the narrator and his fellow traveler are ethically responsible for recognizing and understanding in contemporary terms. They encounter a complex of symptoms whose meanings are not in the past but in future acts of interpretation and analysis. In the anterior act of analysis, the symbolic reality of the nation's racially contested past is brought about, and the specific signifiers the narrator uses—the Spanish "discovery," the Atlanta of the "new South," the Cherokee "dispossession," the "lynching" of Sam Hose, and "slavery"—are imaginary traces whose meanings are not given. This model of historical interpretation may explain the composition of textual and social environments in "Of the Black Belt," and it also suggests why the images constituting these environments are imbued with personal meaning.

The primacy of the past over the present and the immediate can be considered an effect of the weary traveler and his companion's distance from the scenes they contemplate. Yet the travelers do not maintain their distance; they become intimate with the scars on the scenic landscape as they attempt to understand how these came about and what they mean. Throughout *Souls*, the narrator serves as the subject whom the citizen-reader has all along assumed possesses knowledge—namely, about the question "How does it feel to be a problem?" and thus about something that suddenly signifies for the reader. The illusion is that there is someone who already knows the answers to this "question of questions." Despite the illusory nature of this presumed knowledge, access to the knowledge that the reader seeks cannot be had without working through the illusion. Structurally, then, the illusion of "the subject in the know" works like the psychoanalytic transference and is necessary for the traveler-reader's comprehension of the past into which he imaginatively steps.[28] He begins to use that illusion to recognize that he possesses his own knowledge and has already intervened in the scene that he feels he is seeing for the first time (and that echoes the earlier anecdote of the visiting card).

The train, one of the vehicles for the knowledge that comes from this social misrecognition, transports the traveler-reader across a terrain where he might arrive at the final truth he seeks. However, before looking at this, I want to return

---

28. See Jacques Lacan, *The Four Fundamental Concepts of Psychoanalysis: The Seminars of Jacques Lacan, Book XI*, ed. Jacques-Alain Miller, trans. Alan Sheridan (New York: Norton, 1981). Especially see "Of the Subject who is Supposed to Know, of the first Dyad and of the Good," 230–43.

to a moment in the previous section where I analyzed the frustrations of Du Bois's armchair sociologist and his casual observer of the South. Fleshing out his image of the casual observer, the narrator claims that

> the astonished visitor is inclined to ask if after all there is any problem here. But if he lingers long enough there comes the awakening: perhaps in a sudden whirl of passion which leaves him gasping at its bitter intensity; more likely in a gradually dawning sense of things he had not at first noticed. Slowly but surely his eyes begin to catch the shadows of the color-line. . . . He realizes at last that silently, resistlessly, the world about flows by him in two great streams: they ripple on in the same sunshine, they approach and mingle their waters in seeming carelessness,—then they divide and flow apart. It is done quietly; no mistakes are made, or if one occurs, the swift arm of the law and of public opinion swings down for a moment, as when the other day a black man and white woman were arrested for talking together on Whitehall Street in Atlanta.[29]

Du Bois responds to his observer's metaphorical inability to see by transforming the unseen into visual representations. Once again, the "subject who is supposed to know" intervenes on behalf of the reader who is asked to see the critical negativity of not seeing: by not seeing, the reader cannot predict his response beforehand. This shift from necessity to contingency requires that the reader restructure what he confronts and "make it readable in a new way."[30]

This reading in a new way involves pursuing different trajectories and following different lines of flight. For the northern white reader, as I have suggested, this requires reframing, restaging, and re-mediation. This may explain the narrator's suggestion that he and his reader leave the train car from which they initially view the fleeting images of the historic ground of the Black Belt. As they continue their journey through this landscape, one that might embody the truth the reader has been recomposing as he deals with the narrator's statements, he is told:

> If you wish to ride with me you must come into the "Jim Crow Car." There will be little objection,—already four other white men, and a little white girl with her nurse, are in there. Usually the races are mixed in there; but the white coach is all white. Of course this car is not so good as the other, but it is fairly clean and comfortable. The discomfort lies chiefly in the hearts of those four black men yonder—and in mine.[31]

29. Du Bois, *Souls*, 488.
30. For more on how this works, see Slavoj Žižek, *The Sublime Object of Ideology* (London: Verso, 1989), 56.
31. Du Bois, *Souls*, 440–41.

Having already seen some of the textual stratagems used to extend the trope of the author-narrator and reader as figurative fellow travelers, we notice here that the symmetry of four white and four black men and of the two companions, one white and one black, coordinates identifications that create and cut across difference.

Occupying the same place in the train—the vehicle possibly leading to knowledge—and in the National Symbolic has different meanings for each of the travelers as it does for the four white men and the four black men whom the companions observe. The reader is asked to consider these differences as internal to a single symbolic system, as Du Bois continues to pass the "letter" between them. What is more, given the writer's efforts to produce a textual environment that he can control, there is something striking about the narrator's *inability* to vocalize his objections to the racial law of segregation and the color line, about his *refusal* to articulate how difficult he finds it to ignore the personal discomfort of these facts of his life. This incapacity and this resistance are relevant to the entire project of *Souls*. Affective responses such as discomfort, awe, sympathy, and so forth are shown to mediate the social environment that the Veil tropes; moreover, these responses place individuals in unlikely forms of intimate contact such as obtain between our travelers, who potentially exchange and share what they see and feel. This intimacy is figured in the passage quoted above via the black nurse and her white charge.

While the relations among the men on the train are foregrounded in the passage, the relation between the little white girl and her nurse should not be overlooked. An alterist reading of this familiar cultural image of white child and black nurse is unnecessary; what might be more productive is briefly considering how the nurse's body becomes a trope for the intimate and sentimental bonds between black and white. The burden assumed by the black narrator seems to be equivalent to the black nurse's duty of attending to the little girl; however, the similarity ends there, since the body of the nurse in its intimacy with her charge, unlike that of the narrator, is a body that above all else serves an economic function. Additionally, given an interlocutory relationship that is comparable to the one presented in the first chapter of *Souls*, our narrator keeps in mind that his ultimate charge is the narrative task of "tell[ing] in many ways, with loving emphasis and deep . . . detail . . . the striving in the souls of black folk."[32] The love lavished on a story that he "tell[s] again in many ways" is returned via the reader's intimate engagement with that oft-repeated story on which he and the narrator try out various narrative and hermeneutic techniques. The narrator's essential duty in explaining

32. Du Bois, *Souls*, 371.

the Negro problem as coextensive with the white problem requires creating a suitable framework or textual environment, one that produces and uses a racialized picturesque. For the reader, to imagine occupying and acting differently within that frame is no less an essential duty.

A Conclusion on Ruins and Rack Rents

The racial picturesque can finally be extended to two figures—ruins and rack rents. The first of these, the ruin, is a device commonly featured in picturesque texts, drawings, and paintings. But in Du Bois's textual reworking of this element, the ruin recovers social motivation so that political economy is imbricated with its seeming polar opposite, aesthetics. The critique made possible by reading the two together imagines the Black Belt of Georgia pervaded by an atmosphere of decay. The relationship I am describing is obvious in Du Bois's depiction of a ruined plantation, about which he writes, "The half-desolate spirit of neglect born of the very soil seems to have settled on these acres. In times past there were cotton-gins and machinery here; but they have rotted away."[33] How this has come to pass is part of what Du Bois wants his reader to take into account as he tries to provide a different frame for reading the images of a battered southern agrarian economy and relating them to the Negro-white problems.

For instance, the account of white landlords anxious to secure their interests and investments offers another way to interpret the same signs of social and economic hardship that Du Bois brings to light via the racial picturesque. Presenting his side of things, the landowner, whom Du Bois wants his reader to question, "shows his Northern visitor the scarred and wretched land; the ruined mansions, the worn-out soil and mortgaged acres, and says, This is Negro freedom!"[34] The tension between the opposing interpretations of these images ineluctably leads to the conclusion that there is a problem with the South itself. Yet this problem, as with the Negro problem, is not limited to the South, for it encompasses the North as well and indicates that the local and the regional derive their meanings from within the larger contexts of the national and the global.[35] Confronted with

33. Du Bois, *Souls*, 443.
34. Du Bois, *Souls*, 470.
35. In chapter 8, "Of the Quest for the Golden Fleece," Du Bois explains this debt's relationship to American foreign policy: "It is not wholly his fault. The Negro farmer started behind,—started in debt. This was not his choosing, but the crime of this happy go-lucky nation which goes blundering along with its Reconstruction tragedies, its Spanish war interludes and Philippine matinees, just as though God really were dead. Once in debt, it is no easy matter for a whole race to emerge." Du Bois, *Souls*, 466.

the exploitation of farmers in a region that seems infertile and unable to yield anything of value, the reader has to cast about for an explanation of why a people would remain in such a place. Surely this has nothing to do with an inability to sunder connections with the land? Running contrary to this idea, the form of the ruin indicates the kind of change that can occur in social environments that seem most resistant to it.

As for the second element, the rack rent demanded of the tenant farmers brings the notions of value and capital into play with narratological concerns. As previously mentioned, Du Bois has to assume that his reader possesses the requisite cultural capital for enjoying picturesque representation in the first place, but he also has to take it on faith that the reader is willing to consider the ways in which political and social ideas and interests assume their particular forms. With respect to "Of the Black Belt," certain forms are deployed to represent the political and social idea that one cannot take a measure of the South without some sense of how the majority of its people experience life. One of the formal ways in which these lives become palpable for the reader is the personification of debt, not as a mere abstraction but as the most encompassing determinant of the tenant farmers' social and economic existence. The debt, consequent upon the systematic exaction of rack rents, serves the textual function of demonstrating how one class can sustain itself by way of another. This not only brings meaning to the existence of the debt-ridden farmers, it also explains the conditions making possible the values and benefits accruing to the class in possession of the material and cultural capital that the reader himself is also likely to possess.

All this draws lines among text, writer, and reader that define "reality." Remarking social and class distinctions, which are also related to cultural values, only takes us so far with respect to grasping the totality in which these distinctions are determined and their force is recognized. Du Bois's contribution to an analysis of his own social formation and its forces comes about by his making "Of the Black Belt" the centerpiece of *Souls*'s textual reality. The chapter takes from and builds on the topology of the picturesque (its style, figurative diction, personae, and tone) in order to reveal the significance of those individuals considered to be insignificant features in the landscape and to be marginal to the symbolic project that is the United States. Additionally, in registering the affects related to the color line, *Souls* does not vacillate in telling us that the Negro problem is depressing.[36] The

36. My thanks go to my colleague, Jonathan Flatley, who provided me with this phrase and has been generous in sharing his own work on Du Bois and affect.

challenge is for blacks and whites to rouse themselves from the depression that "being" problems, and that "seeing" problems up close, engenders.

Sheila Lloyd teaches African American literary and cultural studies at Wayne State University. She is completing a book manuscript entitled "The Cultural Unconscious: Duty, Attachment, and Desire in African American Transnationalism."

The Double Politics of Double Consciousness: Nationalism and Globalism in *The Souls of Black Folk*

Vilashini Cooppan

During the course of his impressively long life, W. E. B. Du Bois occupied a bewildering range of positions, both on the domestic front of African American politics and on the international front of the anticolonial politics of the emergent Third World. As the recent and widely commemorated centennial of his masterpiece *The Souls of Black Folk* (1903) reminds us, the most influential and ubiquitous African American intellectual and political figure of the twentieth century was also its most penetrating, prescient, and—to this day—haunting anatomist of racial subjectivity. The striking simultaneity with which the outer territories of domestic and world politics converge with the inner territories of psychic life in Du Bois's writings, or with which the evocation of racial nationalism coincides with the invocation of racial globalism, imposes, as few other bodies of work do, the necessity of learning to think doubly about the scene of political identification. Double consciousness, as Du Bois terms the iconic state of

Earlier versions of this essay were presented at the Northwestern University conference "100 Years of *The Souls of Black Folk*: A Celebration," held in October 2003, and at a plenary session dedicated to *Souls* at the American Studies Association conference held in Hartford, Connecticut, in October 2003. I am grateful to Dwight McBride, Robert Gooding-Williams, and Amy Kaplan for inviting me to participate in those events, to my co-panelists and audiences in Evanston and Hartford for spirited debate, and to the editors of this issue of *Public Culture* for their generous and constructive reading of an earlier draft.

Public Culture 17(2): 299–318

"unreconciled strivings" that is both the curse and the gift of African American being, is a case in point: both contemporaneous with what is often characterized as Du Bois's nationalist phase and philosophically coterminous with his career-long effort to think outside the space and time of the nation.[1] Time and again, Du Bois's writings construct nationalism and globalism as neither philosophical antitheses nor chronological others but rather as secret sharers, mutually sustaining conditions of being in whose agonistic embrace lies a quite different story of political evolution than the one we have been accustomed to tell.

Critical studies have narrated a certain passage, even progression, from Du Bois's science to his politics, from his art to his ideology, and from his nationalism to the various globalisms of his pan-Africanism, socialism, communism, Third-Worldism, diasporic consciousness, and most recently what Ross Posnock terms his "cosmopolitan universalism."[2] Conversion narratives, though blessed

1. W. E. B. Du Bois, *The Souls of Black Folk* (New York: Penguin, 1989), 5. Further references to this work will be made parenthetically in the text.

2. Charles U. Smith and Lewis Killian read Du Bois's 1910 departure from Atlanta University and academic sociology for an executive position at the NAACP as the moment when "Du Bois the sociologist had become Du Bois the ideologist of social protest." See Smith and Killian, "Black Sociologists and Social Protest," in *Black Sociologists: Historical and Contemporary Perspectives*, ed. James E. Blackwell and Morris Janowitz (Chicago: University of Chicago Press, 1974), 195. For a related argument, see Elliot Rudwick, "W. E. B. Du Bois as Sociologist," in *Black Sociologists*; and Rudwick, *W. E. B. Du Bois: Voice of the Black Protest Movement* (Urbana: University of Illinois Press, 1982). Another version of this chronological narrative organizes Arnold Rampersad's study *The Art and Imagination of W. E. B. Du Bois* (Cambridge, Mass.: Harvard University Press, 1976), which traces the "vocational tension" between Du Bois's three careers as "historian and sociologist, poet and novelist, and propagandist" (47).

Eric J. Sundquist's comprehensive examination of Du Bois in *To Wake the Nations: Race in the Making of American Literature* (Cambridge, Mass.: Harvard University Press, 1993) updates the narrative, identifying not only a division within Du Bois's writing but also a link, in the form of later works' "completion" of the earlier works' vision (550). In yet another variation on this theme, Cynthia D. Schrager describes the tension and ultimate transition between Du Bois's positivistic social science and his messianic mysticism rooted in late-nineteenth-century spiritualism in "Both Sides of the Veil: Race, Science, and Mysticism in W. E. B. Du Bois," *American Quarterly* 48 (1996): 551–86. Probing the postfoundationalist dimensions of Du Bois's intellectual shifts, Paul Gilroy's *The Black Atlantic: Modernity and Double Consciousness* (Cambridge, Mass.: Harvard University Press, 1993) credits Du Bois with a diasporic cultural politics that resists and even "transcend[s]" the narrow particularisms of racial, ethnic, and national "absolutism" (121). In a similar vein, Ross Posnock's *Color and Culture: Black Writers and the Making of the Modern Intellectual* (Cambridge, Mass.: Harvard University Press, 1998) reads Du Bois as the advocate of a "cosmopolitan universalism" that offers a necessary alternative to cultural studies and its guiding "ideology of 'authenticity'" (21). Thomas C. Holt provides a notable exception to the chronological plot in observing that "Du Bois's paradoxical positions may be taken as somehow emblematic of the African-American experience generally" and by arguing for the "necessarily interactive" relationship of those positions. See Holt's "The Political Uses of Alienation: W. E. B. Du Bois on Politics, Race, and Culture, 1903–1940," *American Quarterly* 42 (1990): 305–6.

with a certain thematic tidiness and chronological certitude, bifurcate at their peril. For as a close reading of Du Bois's writings reveals, he was shaped not just by the transition from one intellectual or political framework to another but also, and possibly more so, by their ongoing contention, collusion, and coexistence. This is the intellectual equivalent of living with double consciousness: sustaining two opposed allegiances, choosing neither, thinking through both. What I want to signal in *Souls*, and Du Bois's work more generally, is a distinct form of national and racial thinking that finds its expressive medium and its oppositional force in a certain kind of globalism. Rather than asserting that Du Bois is more global than national, that his globalism succeeds, transcends, or sublates his nationalism, I suggest, with double consciousness as my model and postcolonial and psychoanalytic theory as my method, that it is only because he is one that he can also be the other.

I take the imbrication of the national and the global to be a hallmark of the analysis we have come to call "postcolonial," an analysis that finds its central method, as the late Edward Said elegantly instructed, in "contrapuntality"—the uncovering of "intertwined and overlapping histories" precisely where there seems to be only a single one; only empire, say, or only resistance, only the national or only the global.[3] I take as another hallmark of the postcolonial a certain temporal disquietude signaled in the much debated "pastness" of the term itself, which prematurely announces the passing of something that remains in forms both residual and resurgent. Just such overlapping of spaces, just such intertwining and haunting of times, distinguish Du Bois's long career. To understand Du Bois through the problematic of the postcolonial is thus not only to hear his thundering voice on the world stage of anti-imperialism, decolonization, and new nationhood; not only to place him in the company of a worldwide revolutionary cadre of black intellectuals like C. L. R. James, Frantz Fanon, and Amilcar Cabral who instantiated the postcolonial era; but equally to detect beneath the surface of Du Bois's global politics the ghostly traces of other affiliations (nation, race) that refuse to die and continually rise to haunt—even where, especially where, they seem no longer to belong. If such palimpsestic work mirrors postcolonial criticism's imperative to read the residues of an imperialism it claims to have bypassed, it equally responds to psychoanalysis's spectral discourse of a past that always returns.[4] This essay

3. Edward W. Said, *Culture and Imperialism* (New York: Knopf, 1993), 18.

4. In contrast to Keith Byerman's assessment of Du Bois as "the wronged son" in his *Seizing the Word: History, Art, and Self in the Work of W. E. B. Du Bois* (Athens: University of Georgia Press, 1994) and Claudia Tate's survey of Du Bois's overdetermined mothers in her *Psychoanalysis and Black Novels: Desire and the Protocols of Race* (New York: Oxford University Press, 1998), I suggest a psychoanalytical approach to Du Bois rooted in the rhetoric of psychic temporality.

seeks to reveal how Du Boisian double consciousness overlaps and intertwines with the identificatory politics of nationalism and globalism; how it deploys distinct ideologies of racial history, racial memory, and the racial psyche to suture nationalism to globalism; and finally, how it enlists certain strategies of narration, especially literary allegory, in order to create a contrapuntal or dialectical formalism that yokes opposites together at the scene of psychopolitical desire.

What Does a Black Man Want? The Double Form of Double Consciousness

First published in the August 1897 issue of the *Atlantic Monthly* under the title "Strivings of the Negro People," reprinted in the first chapter of *Souls*, and famous for a century for its description of the "two warring ideals" of Americanism and Africanism, Du Bois's description of double consciousness can also be read as an account of two contending notions of race. In the broadly evolutionist description with which the well-known passage begins, the Negro comes "after the Egyptian and Indian, the Greek and Roman, the Teuton and Mongolian," a "sort of seventh son" whose fate it is to fall last on the progressive line of Hegelian world history (5). The line of seven coexists here with the agon of two as Du Bois immediately recasts blacks as the possessors of a uniquely double identity, "born with a veil and gifted with second-sight in this American world." Two is in this sense far more than seven, for where seven fixes the meaning of race through apposition, positioning the Negro either as civilization's origin or afterthought, two opens it through opposition to other orders of space, time, and meaning. For all its tragic splitting of the black subject into "an American, a Negro, two souls, two thoughts, two unreconciled strivings; two warring ideals," the oscillating mode of racial twoness refuses to accept their subsequent placing at opposite ends of evolution's line and in separate realms of national life. Double consciousness divides the black subject precisely in order to imagine his eventual "merg[ing]" into a "better and truer self" in which neither half is lost and both coexist: "This, then, is the end of his striving: to be a co-worker in the kingdom of culture, to escape both death and isolation, to husband and use his best powers and his latent genius. These powers of body and mind have in the past been strangely wasted, dispersed, or forgotten. The shadow of a mighty Negro past flits through the tale of Ethiopia the Shadowy and of Egypt the Sphinx" (5–6).

The proleptic time of national belonging, in which it will be "possible for a man to be both a Negro and an American" (5), goes hand in hand with the analeptic time of global longing, in the form of a racial memory that links blacks in America to blacks in Africa. Against the historical depredations of social, spatial, and temporal dislocation (waste, dispersal, forgetting), Du Boisian double consciousness offers a different politics of location, one that restores, reconnects, and remembers in order to lay a different kind of claim to all kinds of territories, both inner and outer. Memory thus functions as a subjective mode of the migrancy that has lately become a defining feature of what might be characterized as the deterritorialized Du Bois—a Du Bois who reaches out to cosmopolitan, diasporic, pan-Africanist, and internationalist affiliations precisely to the extent that he is understood to disassociate himself from particularist and bounded forms of identity, first and foremost national and racial belonging. As migrancy, however, memory directs us not so much *away* from the national-racial particular as out of it and then back again. This is a psychic politics of location in which being national can never be altogether disentangled from feeling global. Reaching outward to Ethiopia and Egypt, the black subject reaches inward into America; accessing a global racial memory, he envisions a different national racial future. Memory's movement readily shuttles the warp of time and the woof of space between the domains of past and future, national and global, individual and collective, in order to weave a new conceptualization and textualization of black identity.

The full force of this model is best grasped in contrast to then-dominant social-scientific discourse, which customarily thought racial identity in terms of evolution. For American sociology in its formative period in the last decades of the nineteenth century and through World War I, social evolutionism's doctrine of progress provided a framework within which to plot the specifically American circumstances of emancipation and urbanization, immigration and assimilation, and racial and ethnic heterogeneity. Widespread acceptance of Herbert Spencer's stagist model of racial development and the Lamarckian tenets he favored, including environmental adaptation and the biological inheritance of acquired characteristics, underwrote calls to restrict the immigration and integration of those ethnic, racial, and national groups considered incapable of adapting to America, progressing beyond "arrested" levels of social and mental development, or ultimately approximating the acceptable forms of citizenship.[5] Du Boisian double consciousness, by contrast, employed a less deterministic, more fluid language to

5. Herbert Spencer, "Progress: Its Law and Cause" (1857), reprinted in Spencer, *Essays on Education and Kindred Subjects* (New York: E. P. Dutton, 1910). On U.S. influence, see John S. Haller, *Outcasts from Evolution: Scientific Attitudes of Racial Inferiority, 1859–1900* (Urbana: University of Illinois Press, 1971), 121–52; George Stocking, *Race, Culture, and Evolution: Essays in the History of Anthropology* (Chicago: University of Chicago Press, 1968), 234–69; and Mark Pittenger, *American Socialists and Evolutionary Thought, 1870–1920* (Madison: University of Wisconsin Press, 1993), 10–26, 240–41.

describe subjective individual and collective experience in a mixed and syncretic society. This is not to say that double consciousness finds freedom from racial evolutionism in race psychology. Double consciousness is not about freedom from one state of being and subsequent entry into another—an essentially chronological plot of identity. Instead, double consciousness presents—and this is its peculiar ontological strength—a state of being defined by the refusal to choose between opposed identities, be it those of the "Negro" and the "American" that the passage describes or those of the contending discourses that subtend its description. I have glossed these discourses as the law of seven and the agon of two, but they might equally be named as the structuring presence of Spencerian social evolutionism and Hegelian historical teleology, on the one hand, and on the other, the "new psychology" propounded by Du Bois's Harvard mentor William James.

James understood the self to be emblematically split, partially "hidden" to itself, and subject to various processes of multiplication, fluctuation, and simultaneity as "fields" and "streams" of consciousness that offered the very obverse of dominant positivist models of internally homogenous and comparatively different races and nations, each fixed at a particular point on history's timeline.[6] Whether James's mystical philosophy of mind provided a template for Du Bois's notion of double consciousness, as several critics suggest;[7] or whether, as David Levering Lewis claims, the "psychic purgatory" of Du Bois's own racial identity was all that was needed to produce a theory of the divided self,[8] one fact remains.

6. See William James, *The Principles of Psychology* (1890; Cambridge, Mass.: Harvard University Press, 1983) and *The Will to Believe and Other Essays in Popular Philosophy* (1897; Cambridge, Mass.: Harvard University Press, 1979), especially "What Psychical Research Has Accomplished." On James as a revolutionary social scientist whose psychological models of mind contradicted deterministic laws of instinct, behavior, heredity, and evolution, see Reba N. Soffer, *Ethics and Society in England: The Revolution in the Social Sciences 1870–1914* (Berkeley: University of California Press, 1978), 32–45, 135–61; Dorothy Ross, *The Origins of American Social Science* (New York: Cambridge University Press, 1991), 239–43; and David Levering Lewis, *W. E. B. Du Bois—Biography of a Race, 1868–1919* (New York: Henry Holt, 1993), 1:87–96. For a useful introduction to the "new psychology" and a discussion of James's contributions, see Robert C. Fuller, *Americans and the Unconscious* (New York: Oxford University Press, 1986), especially chaps. 3, 4.

7. On James's influence on Du Bois, see Rampersad, *Art and Imagination*, 68–90; Sundquist, *To Wake the Nations*, 571–72; Posnock, *Color and Culture*, 10–11, 18–19, 35–36, and 57–58; Dickson D. Bruce, "W. E. B. Du Bois and the Idea of Double Consciousness," *American Literature* 64 (1992): 299–309; Thomas J. Otten, "Pauline Hopkins and the Hidden Self of Race," *ELH* 59 (1992): 227–56; and Shamoon Zamir, *Dark Voices: W. E. B. Du Bois and American Thought, 1888–1903* (Chicago: University of Chicago Press, 1995), 153–68. Du Bois himself describes his debt to James in *Dusk of Dawn: An Essay toward an Autobiography of a Race Concept* (1940; New York: Schocken, 1968), 578, 590, 770–71.

8. Levering Lewis, *W. E. B. Du Bois—Biography of a Race*, 1:96.

Du Bois's unique anatomy of racial and panracial, national and global identifications, its doubled simultaneity nowhere better distilled than in the description of
double consciousness, found expression there in what we cannot fail to recognize
as a concept of the racial psyche, however much we may question its sources and
origins. Through the construct of the racial psyche—internally divided, linked
outside itself, endlessly moving between the space and time of the self and that of
the other—Du Bois elaborates the broadly connective thinking for which *Souls*
and his later works are justly famous. As Du Bois's earliest and most lasting
articulation of the idea of the racial psyche, double consciousness provides both
the ground and the figure, the philosophical condition and the expressive modality, of his double politics.

In a stringent counterargument to the one just outlined, Adolph Reed charges
that the idea of double consciousness "by and large disappeared from Du Bois's
writing after 1903." Citing Du Bois's acknowledgment in the subsequent year
of August Weismann's rediscovery of Mendelian genetics, Reed concludes that
by 1904 Du Bois "had begun revising his thinking about race in ways that were
incompatible with the neo-Lamarckian resonances surrounding the double consciousness idea."[9] In Reed's narrative, the idea left behind by Du Bois has been
perversely reanimated by several generations of political historians, psycholo-
gists, philosophers, and literary critics in order to serve their own purposes, rang-
ing from 1920s integrationism to 1960s nationalism and 1980s academic race
theory. Scholars in the last group warrant Reed's most severe criticism for having
disconnected double consciousness from the intellectual history of early-twentieth-century social science and Progressive Era politics, only to dubiously link it
through "assertions and intimations," "inference" and conjecture, to other intellectual genealogies, notably the work of G. W. F. Hegel, Ralph Waldo Emerson,
Josiah Royce, and most of all William James, in an effort to foreground the psychological dimensions of Du Bois's idea.[10]

9. Adolph Reed, *W. E. B. Du Bois and American Political Thought: Fabianism and the Color
Line* (New York: Oxford University Press, 1997), 124. Reed refers to "Heredity and the Public
Schools," Du Bois's 1904 lecture to the Principals' Association of the Colored Schools of Washing-
ton, D.C., reprinted in *Pamphlets and Leaflets by W. E. B. Du Bois*, ed. Herbert Aptheker (White
Plains, N.Y.: Kraus-Thomson, 1986), 45–52.

10. Reed, *American Political Thought*, 105 and n. 80, 98 and n. 44. On Hegel's influences on
Du Bois, Reed cites Gilroy, *Black Atlantic*, 134; Joel Williamson, *The Crucible of Race: Black-
White Relations in the American South since Emancipation* (New York: Oxford University Press,
1984); Robert Gooding-Williams, "Philosophy of History and Social Critique in *The Souls of Black
Folk*," *Social Science Information* 26 (1987): 106–8; and Jacqueline Stevens, "Beyond Tocqueville,
Please!" *American Political Science Review* 89 (1995): 987–90. On the collected influence of James,

Certainly Du Bois's understanding of race at the time of *Souls* was that of a turn-of-the-century American social scientist, described by George Stocking as hereditarian, Lamarckian, and convinced that "complex cultural phenomena were carried in the 'blood,' if only as 'instincts' or 'temperamental proclivities.' "[11] And certainly there are clear traces of this social evolutionism, and the curiously biologized notion of culture and identity it underwrote, in the notion of double consciousness. If, however, we read double consciousness as it teaches us to read, we cannot see it as purely the product of social evolutionist thinking but rather as a notion locked in a dialogue between that thinking and some emergent alternative. That alternative is variously sociohistorical, sociocultural, even psychocultural with regard to what race is, and variously national and global with regard to where race is situated. If we wish furthermore to avoid recasting the evolution of Du Bois's understanding of race as an altogether too tidy passage from biology to culture, a chronological conversion narrative of the sort I have argued against, we have to go back to double consciousness and see that what it describes—the condition of contending opposites—is also what it is. In other words, double consciousness demands the discernment not only of its famously warring identities ("an American, a Negro"), but equally of a set of competing and colluding discourses—the biological and the cultural, the social and the psychic, the material and the metaphoric, the historical and the spiritual, the national and the global, the forward-moving plot of racial progress and the backward-moving gaze of racial memory, all paradoxically, explosively, condensed into the fraught figure of the black man in America.

Perhaps it is the distillation of so much into so little that explains the staying power of double consciousness in twentieth-century scholarship on black politics, literature, and culture. Such rhetorical overdetermination and conceptual excess implicitly demand that we grasp, or forge, connections between seemingly separate discourses, ideas, even zones and times of existence.[12] Double consciousness,

Royce, and Emerson on Du Bois, Reed cites Rampersad, *Art and Imagination*, 74; Sundquist, *To Wake the Nations*, 487, 570–71; Bruce, "W. E. B. Du Bois and the Idea of Double Consciousness," 304; Kimberly Benston, "I Yam What I Am: The Topos of (Unnaming) in Afro-American Literature," *Black Literature and Literary Theory*, ed. Henry Louis Gates Jr. (New York: Oxford University Press, 1984), 170; Werner Sollors, *Beyond Ethnicity: Consent and Descent in American Culture* (New York: Oxford University Press, 1986), 186–88, 249; and Cornel West, *The American Evasion of Philosophy: A Genealogy of Pragmatism* (Madison: University of Wisconsin Press, 1989), 142–43.

11. Stocking, *Race, Culture, and Evolution*, 251, 256.

12. Thus, where Reed advocates for the "synchronic focus" of contextualizing Du Bois's thinking within that of his peers and his moment, as opposed to the "diachronic telescopy" that he under-

then, is not only the specter haunting black studies but also the ghostly image of a critical method that the field simply cannot live after or without. This method, less conjectural than conjunctural,[13] is as germane to black studies as to post-colonial and psychoanalytic studies. All three, I think, can benefit from serious consideration of Du Bois through the lenses of migrancy and memory. This is not a Du Bois imperialistically annexed by the respective concerns of postcolonialism and psychoanalysis, but rather a Du Bois with something to say to those and other critical fields and perhaps even with some way to renew them. Du Bois gives to postcolonial studies a figure in which, contrary to the thrust of much recent argument, nationalism and racialism did not give way to a hybrid, cosmopolitan, globalism but rather coexisted alongside and in some profound sense through it. With regard to psychoanalytic theory, Du Bois (like Fanon) offers a model of the psyche deeply embedded in the most material questions of racial, national, and global identity. If *Souls* is something like our collective critical conscience, a haunting reminder of the half-finished project of racial equality and of the intellectual's responsibility to advance it, it is equally, or could become, our collective critical model. Reading *Souls*, I suggest, we may learn how to speak the pull of the particular and the push of the universal in the same breath.

Double Consciousness and Dialectical Formalism

The fact that Du Bois was thinking race, at the time of *Souls* as throughout his career, through a multiplicity of discourses, some inherited, others invented, none

stands to mark interpretations that advance "putative chain[s] of influence," I would urge a reading that thinks through both axes and even through their convergence. Reed, *American Political Thought*, 107, n. 80.

13. I take the model of conjunctural analysis from Antonio Gramsci's reconceptualization of history as a series of kaleidoscopic movements in which distinct subsets of dominant and subaltern classes now join or "articulate" at their points of commonality to produce hegemony, now break apart along their differences to produce change. As usefully glossed by Stuart Hall, Gramsci's theory of articulation rethinks the units and methods of social analysis in terms of positionality—from his rewriting of the concept of the ruling class, unified in itself and in its action, into brokered, constellated, constantly renegotiated historic blocs; to his redrawing of history's line as conjuncture's pattern and his reimagining of the nation-state as, in Hall's words, "not a *thing* to be seized, overthrown or 'smashed' with a single blow, but a complex *formation* in modern societies which must become the focus of a number of different strategies and struggles because it is an arena of different social contestations." Hall, "Gramsci's Relevance for the Study of Race and Ethnicity," *Journal of Communication Inquiry* 10, no. 2 (1986): 19. As I understand it, a conjunctural analysis of Du Bois explores how nationalism and globalism, gender and race, sociology and psychology, the line of progress and the agonistic dyad of doubleness all come together and break apart in order to produce social and conceptual change.

of them wholly independent of the others, argues for a more connective, conjunctural, or contrapuntal approach to his writing. By way of example, I consider another passage from the first chapter of *Souls*. As Reed disapprovingly notes, only a few pages after his opening description of racial twoness, Du Bois appears to shortchange the darker half by describing Emancipation's optimistic vision of equality as "the dreams of a credulous race-childhood" (11). The phrase, like so many found in Du Bois's writing, is blatantly paternalistic and elitist, worthy of Spencer, Freud, Hegel, or any other great primitivist, and clearly embedded in the very developmentalist narratives Du Bois is purportedly trying to denounce. Yet if we follow the phrase through the entire passage (as Reed does not), something rather different emerges. Referring back to Emancipation's vision of equalities to come, "physical freedom, political power, the training of brains and the training of hands," and asking "Are they all wrong,—all false?" Du Bois responds: "No, not that, but each alone was over-simple and incomplete,—the dreams of a credulous race-childhood or the fond imaginings of the other world which does not know and does not want to know our power" (11).

This passage's formal claim for a combined strategy of equality that will unite bodily integrity under the law, the exercise of the ballot box, and the opportunity of the classroom is also a claiming of form. As such, the passage provides an exemplary instance of the yoked structure on which Du Bois's thinking of race and nation so frequently depended. So in a sentence that is itself a locked embrace of opposites, one race's dreams of equality are another's simultaneous desire and fear, recognized in "fond imagining" precisely because they are denied in fact. For all its seeming initial allegiance to the developmentalist doctrines of social evolutionism, the law of seven, the sentence is nonetheless much more indebted to the agon of two, that drama of interlocked self and other that is both the dream and the nightmare of difference. That the sentence references the most material of facts—freedom, power, education—in the language of dream, fantasy, and inner life argues not for its betrayal of double consciousness's account of race (its abandonment of the split race-man and return to the credulous race-child of social-scientific custom) but rather for an ongoing echo of double consciousness's central feature—namely, its doubling of the thing it describes and the form in which it does so, what I call dialectical formalism. "To think dialectically," explains Fredric Jameson, "is to invent a space from which to think . . . two identical yet antagonistic features together all at once."[14] *Souls*'s oft-cited

14. Fredric Jameson, *The Political Unconscious: Narrative as a Socially Symbolic Act* (Ithaca, N.Y.: Cornell University Press, 1981), 234.

polydiscursivity is in this sense the dialectical form of double consciousness writ large—a persistent twinning of such seemingly opposed yet intimately entwined idioms as the sociological and the literary, the ethnographic and the psychological, the cultural and the economic, the political and the personal, the prophetic and the elegiac, the manifesto and the memoir, and perhaps most famously, the juxtaposed fragments of European poetry and slave sorrow songs that open every chapter. All of these, the text seems to imply, are as necessary as the overarching metaphor of double consciousness in order to represent the "strange meaning of being black here in the dawning of the Twentieth Century" (1).

Double consciousness is clearly too double for singularizing interpretation, too intimately connected to other social discourses and material histories to be simply reduced to a purely psychological figure of split subjectivity or a psychic rhetoric of temporality. But to altogether dismiss the psychic resonances is to miss something fundamental about Du Bois's politics. What we have been accustomed to think of as doubleness might equally be understood as the multiplicity and connectivity of a politics that constantly reaches outside a set of bounded norms (nation and race foremost among them) toward more unbounded definitions of those very norms. If nation and race subsequently expand, deterritorialize, and move, whether in the discrete example of double consciousness or in *Souls* more broadly, they do so in no small part because of their subjection to the category of memory in particular and the psyche in general.

Thomas J. Otten credits the popular dissemination of spiritualism and Jamesian psychology with providing late-nineteenth-century American culture with what he calls "the sort of analytical plot that we now think of as Freudian," in which a "hidden" or lost part of the self can be accessed and brought to the surface of consciousness through the work of memory. Such painstaking reconstruction aims at once to restore the past, to work through it, and to move beyond it in the interest of someday living differently.[15] It is the particular genius of double consciousness to produce Du Bois's own version of such an "analytic plot," within which he has recourse to a particular kind of time (racial memory and racial history, troped, as Otten points out, as Africa) in order to then lay claim to a different kind of racial space—not the divided world of Jim Crow America but that utopian space of belonging within which "it might be possible for a man to be both a Negro and an American." Du Bois's use of this "plot" need not make him a black James

15. Otten, "Pauline Hopkins," 229. For a related argument see Susan Gillman, *Blood Talk: American Race Melodrama and the Culture of the Occult* (Chicago: University of Chicago Press, 2003), 148–99.

or, if we want to entertain a notion for which there is even less evidence, a black Freud. To argue so would be to grossly misrepresent Du Bois's profound achievements and to caricature the kind of critical method I am calling for. More then simply seeing psychic resonances in the notion of double consciousness, more than reconstructing the path of influence by which those resonances got there, this method explores what cognitive work the discourse of the racial psyche performs in a given articulation of nationalism and to what political aspirations and textual strategies it is allied.

In the emblematic case of double consciousness, the travails of a masculine racial psyche split on the terrain of national belonging ("an American, a Negro") are set within the feminized and fantasized geographies of Ethiopia the Shadowy and Egypt the Sphinx as places of recuperation and restoration. Egypt the Sphinx is both a racial memory, a form of time that returns the African American subject to its forgotten origin, and a distinctly diasporic space, a reminder that for some subjects it is only by going outside the national, only by inhabiting alternative kinds of space and time, that they can lay claim to a nation that variously anteriorizes or exteriorizes them on the forward-moving line of progress. The final pages of *Souls* similarly turn to the extranational space-time of world history in order to make the point that the place currently occupied by blacks on the timeline of progress cannot be where they are doomed to remain and is not even where they always were.

> The silently growing assumption of this age is that the probation of races is past, and that the backward races of today are of proven inefficiency and not worth the saving. Such an assumption is the arrogance of peoples irreverent toward Time and ignorant of the deeds of men. A thousand years ago such an assumption would have made it difficult for the Teuton to prove his right to life. Two thousand years ago such dogmatism, readily welcome, would have scouted the idea of blond races ever leading civilization. So wofully unorganized is sociological knowledge that the meaning of progress, the meaning of "swift" and "slow" in human doing, and the limits of human perfectability, are veiled, unanswered sphinxes on the shores of science. (214)

For American proslavery scientists of the second half of the nineteenth century, ancient Egypt was a once Caucasian, now diluted and degenerate, nation in which blacks were understood to have occupied their appropriate places as slaves and servants. But for Du Bois and his Ethiopianist contemporaries, Egypt was the very bedrock of black history, and the stone sphinx was perhaps its most privileged symbol.[16] Blacks' claim to recognition as a race decidedly "worth the saving" rests in Du Bois's account on two familiar tactics. The first of these depends on dialectical inversion (what blacks are now is what Teutons once were). The second of these deploys a rhetoric of temporality that looks outside the moment and place of the present in order to anticipate a different future. Here, as in many of his other writings, Du Bois can be seen to share with early sociology, anthropology, psychology, and psychoanalysis a complex negotiation of race and time that marshals developmentalist plots of identity and history only to simultaneously disrupt them by reference to what (or whom) they leave behind or fail to remember.[17] These remainders, of which *Souls* is a veritable catalog, return to ghost progress with its others.

The sphinxes that flank *Souls'* beginning and end thus replace the inherently racialized timeline of progress with an alternative haunted iconography and chronology of race. Via a version of history that relies not on chronological sequence but rather on the temporal oscillation and geographical convergence associated with the work of the racial psyche, Du Bois's sphinxes are made to break away from their "own" place on the world-historical timeline and instead install the imaginative connection that brings Egypt, the territory of racial memory, to America, the territory of national belonging. Finally, in their ultimate appearance in *Souls* as in their first, the Egyptian sphinxes are a form of time (memory) and of space (diaspora) that connects divergent points as well as a mode of representation that itself takes linkage through movement as its animating principle. In other words, the sphinxes are allegories. It is in this form that they reveal the inner logic of double consciousness and its double politics.

Memory's Textuality: The Psychic Work of Allegory

"Herein lie buried many things which if read with patience may show the strange meaning of being black here in the dawning of the Twentieth Century" (1). So begins the "Forethought" to *Souls*. History in Du Bois is that which has been

16. For a discussion of Egypt as one of Du Bois's "signature sites" and its conceptual "multivalence," see Gillman, *Blood Talk*, 186–99. For historical accounts of the uses of Egypt in dominant Euro-American racial discourse, see Martin Bernal, *Black Athena: The Afroasiatic Roots of Classical Civilization* (New Brunswick, N.J.: Rutgers University Press, 1987); and Robert Young, "Egypt in America: *Black Athena*, Racism and Colonial Discourse," in *Racism, Modernity, and Identity: On the Western Front*, ed. Ali Rattansi and Sallie Westwood (Cambridge, U.K.: Polity, 1994).

17. For a provocative discussion of race and time, see Charles Lemert, "The Race of Time: Du Bois and Reconstruction," *boundary 2* 27, no. 3 (2000): 215–48.

"buried" and must therefore surface, like the "repressed and buried reality of this fundamental history" in whose "restor[ation] to the surface of the text" Jameson finds the function of the political unconscious (20). Du Bois's history rises up in the ghostly forms of racial memory and in the promise of a racial future yet to be redeemed. Such oscillating time is the proper domain of allegory, the literary mode that is perhaps more than any other history's equivalent. Allegory traditionally denotes a form of interpretation in which two parallel, temporally distinct levels of signification are read in such a way that one is understood to provide the key to the other. "Allegories," writes Walter Benjamin, "are, in the realm of thoughts, what ruins are in the realm of things."[18] Allegory thus marks the formal presence of a particular kind of time in which the past outlives itself, a time that demands that the subject return to the past as it surges into, even becomes contemporaneous with, the present. Benjamin calls "medieval" the style of allegory that persistently closes the gap between past and present, history and future, the first level of signification and the second. By contrast, "baroque" allegory exploits that gap, finding within it the occasion of a character Benjamin calls "dialectical" (171). The doubled or dialectical moment of allegorical return has a talismanic force in *Souls* from the Egyptian sphinx onward and in fact forms one of the text's leitmotifs. In allegory's function we see again double consciousness's work of double reading, carried forward in a formal medium that is itself the expression or, in Jamesonian terms, the structural displacement of an unconscious both political *and* racial. Allegory, in other words, is how the racial psyche writes itself in *Souls*.

Within the classical medieval-religious form of allegory to which *Souls* is so powerfully indebted, "Egypt" denotes bondage and implies a freedom to come in the prefigurative fulfillment of time. It is in this sense that chapter 7 of *Souls* describes Georgia's rural Dougherty County, in the heart of the Black Belt, as "the Egypt of the Confederacy," home to "perhaps the richest slave kingdom the modern world ever knew" (100–101). Now, Du Bois remarks, the land is a mere echo of its former self, a ghostly geography of phantoms, remnants, and ruins that serves as a reminder that all that was once there was "built upon a groan" (102). As this chapter and the following one make clear in their portraits of the devastating poverty of sharecropping, wage labor, and tenancy, passage from the second Egypt has brought only destroyed dreams, broken promises, "the slavery of debt" (128), and the recapitulation of that which had supposedly been left

18. Walter Benjamin, "Allegory and *Trauerspiel*," in *The Origins of German Tragic Drama*, trans. John Osborne (London: New Left Books, 1977), 177–78.

behind. In contrast to medieval allegory's temporal teleology of prefiguration and fulfillment, the circular rhythms of a slavery that never ends signal the presence of a different kind of allegory, one indebted less to eschatology's time than to memory's, that same time that I have argued structures Du Bois's racial psyche and enables its historical and political life.

In Du Bois, as in Benjamin and Jameson, allegory is the vehicle of history. In Du Bois's case, allegory is furthermore what allows for history's double cast: in the Benjaminian mode of ruin, as the cause of the decay and disorganization that haunts the racial subject; and in the Jamesonian mode of revolution, as the very means of that subject's deliverance. What the lived history of slavery's ruination and Jim Crow's deprivation take away, the remembered history of Ethiopia the Shadowy and Egypt the Sphinx will restore, in the fulfillment and fullness of a time when it will be possible to be both Negro and American, both American and African, and, if we look toward Du Bois's later politics, both African American and part of a global color line that "belts the world." Perhaps the necessary interdependence of history's two levels—history as what is lived and history as what is remembered or redeemed—is what it finally means to imagine history as allegory, that is, as a form of representation whose two levels or two selves are not chronologically sequenced or hierarchically positioned so much as deeply imbricated with or articulated to one another. History in this sense is itself a form of double consciousness.

To understand the dialectical nature of historical allegory in Du Bois and, furthermore, to isolate the raced and gendered material that provides its symbolic content, it will be helpful to consider yet another critical voice. Paul de Man's 1969 essay "The Rhetoric of Temporality" returned to Benjamin's "Allegory and *Trauerspiel*" in order to present allegory not as history's double but rather as its rhetorical fantasy. For de Man, allegory is how history misreads itself. Unlike irony ("the mode of the present"), allegory "exists entirely within an ideal time that is never here and now but always a past or an endless future." Thus, "irony is a synchronic structure, while allegory appears as a successive mode capable of engendering duration as the illusion of a continuity that it knows to be illusionary."[19] As the rhetorical mode that, in de Man's words, "takes us back to the predicament of the conscious subject" (a subject he also describes as "a

19. Paul de Man, "The Rhetoric of Temporality," in *Blindness and Insight: Essays in the Rhetoric of Contemporary Criticism* (Minneapolis: University of Minnesota Press, 1983), 187–228, 226. For an excellent reading of this essay and Benjamin's, and a supple theory of national allegory, see Doris Sommer, *Foundational Fictions: The National Romances of Latin America* (Berkeley: University of California Press, 1991), chap. 1.

divided self"),[20] irony is *Souls*'s preferred register for describing the conflicts of an explicitly racialized, implicitly masculinized double consciousness. Recall, for example, chapter 4's concluding lament: "How shall man measure Progress there where the dark-faced Josie lies? How many heartfuls of sorrow shall balance a bushel of wheat? How hard a thing is life to the lowly, and yet how human and real! And all this life and love and strife and failure,—is it the twilight of nightfall or the flush of some faint-dawning day? Thus sadly musing, I rode to Nashville in the Jim Crow car" (62). In this passage allegory belongs to Josie, irony to Du Bois. A similar gendered division of labor structures the description of double consciousness, which yokes the divided racial subject's strictly ironic apprehension of "a peculiar sensation . . . this sense of always looking at one's self through the eyes of others, of measuring one's soul by the tape of a world that looks on in amused contempt and pity" to the imaginary territories of an America to come and an Ethiopia and Egypt that were—forms of allegorical time expressed in feminized bodies and geographies. Though *Souls* is punctuated, often piercingly, by an irony that details the sudden falling of the veil over one who imagines he has risen above it, the text is more indebted to the diachronic sweep of allegory, in which it finds the mirror image of its unceasing temporal fluctuations between a distant racial history and a racial future to come.

True to allegory's refusal to occupy a single moment in time (de Man's "here and now"), Du Boisian allegory resists redistricting of all kinds. In Jameson's now notorious formula, "all third-world texts are necessarily . . . allegorical, and in a very specific way: they are to be read as what I will call *national allegories*."[21] In Aijaz Ahmad's forceful critique, Jameson's model of allegory tends toward totalization, employing the inherently flattening discourse of "Three Worlds Theory" in order to argue, in Ahmad's words, "the proposition that the 'Third World' is a *singular* formation, possessing its own unique, unitary force of determination in the sphere of ideology (nationalism) and cultural production (the national allegory)."[22] Du Boisian double consciousness argues against the position ventriloquized by Ahmad, against the notion that one could ever limn identity without reaching beyond the singular and toward the double. Reading the rhetoric of double consciousness, in which nation always lies alongside globe and national allegory regularly employs global form—from the positivists' timeline

20. De Man, "The Rhetoric of Temporality," 222.

21. Fredric Jameson, "Third-World Literature in the Era of Multinational Capitalism," *Social Text* 15 (1986): 69.

22. Aijaz Ahmad, "Jameson's Rhetoric of Otherness and the National Allegory," in *In Theory: Classes, Nations, Literatures* (New York: Verso, 1992), 119.

of world history to the alternative time of cross-continental racial memory—thus teaches us to see allegory, as much as the history to which allegory points, in double form. By this logic, allegory, even the subset of "Third World allegory," cannot be "always" national. For allegory is never just one thing but always both that thing and its dialectical double. This is also to say, as Benjamin and de Man suggest, that allegory makes its meaning through its movement. Building on their arguments for allegory as a species of historical consciousness (Benjamin) or *méconnaissance* (de Man), both of which emphasize allegory as a rhetoric of temporality, I suggest that allegory's temporal movement underwrites its capacity to narrate spatial movement, in particular the movement between the national and the global.[23] This is the movement that structures double consciousness and later provides the organizing pattern for *Darkwater* (1920), *Dark Princess* (1928), and *Black Reconstruction* (1935).

Conclusion

It is relatively easy to discern *Souls*'s debt to the nineteenth century's favored explanatory mechanism, the timeline of progress. And it is strikingly clear that Du Bois's simultaneous adoption and disruption of that narrative was the sign of someone who was using the conceptual tools of his moment in order to change its understanding of African Americans. This essay has begun to explore the presence in *Souls* of other, more uncertain and mobile modalities of time *and* space. To the extent that Du Bois's consciousness of nation, race, and globe were all entwined (perhaps nowhere more concisely than in *Souls*'s description of double consciousness), a conjunctural analysis would want to ask at what specific points and by what means they are joined together. Certainly race itself provides a suture, thanks to its double meaning as both the shattering source of division, difference, and discrimination within the nation and the redemptive site of memory, connection, and affiliation across the globe. It has been my further contention that *Souls* turns to two additional modes in order to link nation, race, and globe. First, *Souls* deploys a certain kind of time for which the psyche, with its recursive temporality

23. Jameson's essay later turns to the possibilities of allegorical movement, citing "the capacity of allegory to generate a range of distinct meanings or messages, simultaneously, as the allegorical tenor and vehicle change places." Jameson, "Third-World Literature," 74. Although I cannot rehearse the argument fully here, suffice it to say that Jameson's literary theorizing of what he calls "the allegorical spirit" ("profoundly discontinuous, a matter of breaks and heterogeneities, of the multiple polysemia of the dream rather than the homogenous representation of the symbol," 73), works against the broader totalizing claims of his essay.

of memory, at once backward-looking and forward-moving, provides a model. Second, *Souls* enlists a certain literary figure, allegory, that is also characterized by a back-and-forth movement between two orders of time, space, and signification. If psychic space-time finds condensation in the resolutely masculine figure of double consciousness's "two warring ideals in one dark body, whose dogged strength alone keeps it from being torn asunder," allegory on the other hand is persistently linked to the female and feminized bodies that litter *Souls*—from dark Josie left behind by the forces of Progress; to the slave mother, that "figur[e] of the present-past" who, along with the Southern gentleman, "ever stands to typify that day [of Emancipation] to coming ages" (26); to the relentlessly feminized compromiser Booker T. Washington; and, of course, to the female figures of Ethiopia the Shadowy and Egypt the Sphinx. The expansive geography of a masculinized racial psyche can thus be seen to depend on allegory's gendered substratum, just as the far-flung coordinates of Du Bois's globalism are subtended by his nationalism.

Such a reading orients us differently to the question of Du Bois's nationalism, so often understood as the prelude to his globalism. Reaching backward to Ethiopia the Shadowy and Egypt the Sphinx, voicing the claims of racial history and racial memory, allows Du Bois's Negro to reach up and into an America that would exclude him. Double consciousness thus describes a psychic time that is simultaneously a political space; a time whose back-and-forth movement provides the measure of a nationalism and globalism that can never be plotted on a timeline of ideological progress (nationalism first, globalism after). Double consciousness is also emphatically not the assimilationist plot of racial identity *becoming* national identity, another chronological progression from one autonomous entity to another. Rather, double consciousness attempts to understand race, nation, and globe in terms of the quite different spatiotemporal plot of simultaneity. Race and nation, nation and globe are in this sense not constituted "before" or "after," "inside" or "outside" each other. Rather, they coexist in a mutually sustaining fluctuation between seemingly opposed yet secretly conjoined states of being. This process is analogous in its work to what Nahum Dimitri Chandler has called the "economy of desedimentation," by which he understands a process in which a previously essentialized category, namely "race," is at once used and altered, deployed and evacuated, in such a way as to "elaborate a sense of being that in itself could not be reduced to some simple essence."[24] Race as Du Bois imagines

24. Nahum Dimitri Chandler, "The Economy of Desedimentation: W. E. B. Du Bois and the Discourses of the Negro," *Callaloo* 19 (1996): 80, 85.

it and nation as he articulates it (both in the expressive sense of giving it voice and the Gramscian sense of linking or constellating it to other categories of being and global constituencies of affiliation) are not reduced to the fixed typology of essence, the status of being one thing. Instead, race and nation expand to be several things simultaneously. It is this expansion and simultaneity that characterize Du Boisian space-time most broadly and allow him to sustain, in _Souls_ and subsequently, a distinctly doubled or desedimented sense of race and nation. Without it, neither his nationalism nor his globalism could have come into being.

The model of a nationalism always already inflected by globalism and of a globalism that cannot help but return to the scene of nationalism stands to change our evaluation both of Du Bois's politics and of the textual forms in which we have read those politics. For example, we might begin to think differently about the apparent paradox of _Souls_'s turn to a markedly global, cosmopolitan language in order to express its unique brand of African American nationalism. Defined as an ideology of border crossing, cosmopolitanism shapes _Souls_'s vision of history (in which ancient Egypt, precolonial Africa, and early-twentieth-century America are all linked in a racial continuum), of literature (in which the ideal free black subject can aspire, as Du Bois himself does, to sit with Shakespeare and Aurelius "above the veil"), and indeed of literary form itself (_Souls_ is notable for the border crossing of its multidisciplinary, polygeneric form). But this cosmopolitanism of form in _Souls_ does not necessarily imply a related bypassing or transcendence of nationalist identification. Allegory, I have suggested, is the formal expression of the conjoined nationalism and globalism that is the political unconscious of _Souls_. So, too, might _Souls_'s cosmopolitan form be said to be the symptom or trace of the globalism its border-crossing style mirrors and of the nationalism implicit within and inextricable from that globalism. Seen in this way, _Souls_ is a different kind of founding text. National in its address, diasporic in its form, and marked throughout by processes of movement, be they those of migrancy, memory, or the allegory that is their textual double, _Souls_ emerges as the kind of text that both grounds a tradition and keeps it moving.

To return to the idea that has been my major concern, one could argue that double consciousness has a second life in Du Bois's career-spanning figure of the color line, which is also emblematically racial, national, and global, both dividing (as the line of racial discrimination within the nation) and connecting (as the line of panracial affiliation that "belts the world"). It is equally possible to read Du Bois's career-spanning strategy of allegory as inheriting the mantle of double consciousness, allegory as the long formal shadow of the new kind of thinking about race, nation, and globe that double consciousness gestures toward.

317

Unpacking this textual process, showing how and why nationalism and globalism are linked together, teaches us something about how to read Du Bois and about how he teaches us to read. The reading strategies that Du Bois's oeuvre elicits, even demands, are contrapuntal, conjunctural, and, quite simply, *big*. We always knew we had to think big (and read close) with Du Bois; we just didn't know how much.

Vilashini Cooppan teaches literature at the University of California at Santa Cruz. Her essays on postcolonial and world literatures, globalization theory, psychoanalysis, and nationalism have appeared in *Symploke*, *Comparative Literature Studies*, and several published and forthcoming edited volumes. She is completing a book manuscript entitled "Inner Territories: Fictions and Fantasms of the Nation in Postcolonial Writing."

The Grooves of Temporality

Alexander G. Weheliye

This essay takes W. E. B. Du Bois's *The Souls of Black Folk* (1903) as a model of modern black temporality and cultural practice rooted in and routed through the sonic. While *Souls* blends together history, eulogy, sociology, personal anecdote, economics, lyricism, ethnography, fiction, and cultural criticism of black music, Du Bois's central aesthetic achievement in this epochal text appears in bars of music placed before each chapter. The way the "Sorrow Songs" are threaded throughout the text is the key to *Souls*'s sonorous ignition. Besides the musical epigraphs, references to hearing and the "Sorrow Songs" close both the "Forethought" and "Afterthought," underpinning the manuscript both graphically—through musical notes—and in its content—through Du Bois's theorization of black music's place in U.S. and world culture. When Du Bois ([1903] 1989: 2; emphasis mine) first introduces the "Sorrow Songs" in the "Forethought," he links them directly to the souls of black folk: "Before each chapter, as now printed, stands a bar of the Sorrow Songs—some echo of haunting melody from the only American music, which welled up from *black souls* in the dark past." Moreover, in the "Afterthought" to *Souls*, Du Bois ([1903] 1989: 217) asks his readers to "Hear [his] cry," and the best way to *hear* the souls of black folk, as Du Bois remarks at the end of chapter 1 ("Of Our Spiritual Strivings"), is to listen to the "Sorrow Songs." Du Bois ([1903] 1989: 12) does not ask his readers to view or see the souls of black folk, but instead he writes so "that men may listen to the souls of black folk." Much in the same way that Du Bois appeals to the ear in his

Public Culture 17(2): 319–38
Copyright © 2005 by Duke University Press

theory of double consciousness, this injunction to imagine blackness sonically provides a phono-graphic guidepost for reading and hearing *Souls*.

Contemporary critics agree that the sonic signs taken from the Western tradition of musical notation cannot form a mimetic merger with spirituals. Eric Sundquist (1993: 470), for instance, states that "the musical epigraphs are . . . an example of a cultural 'language' that cannot be properly interpreted, or even 'heard' at all, since it fails to correspond to the customary mapping of sounds and signs that make up the languages of the dominant (in this case white) culture." Of course, these notes were also unable to faithfully reproduce the Western classical music for which they were originally designed; for example, they cannot capture the full range of a performance of a Bach fugue, since the piece will be interpreted and performed differently depending on who plays it and when and where it is staged. As Alan Durant (1984: 98) has argued, "Notation marks an ordering of bodily movements of musical performance in addition to immediate verbal directives, and provided historically the possibility for pieces of music of a specialized, if restricted, kind of permanence. In this sense, notation was one necessary condition to take on, as composition, a temporal and aesthetic independence from particular versions and collaborations of its realization." By incorporating musical notes into his text as doubles for spirituals, Du Bois attempts to make the musical works that comprise this body independent of their performances and locations in history while also ensconcing them in new forms of contextual codependency. Instead of being placed within a particular historical framework, the spirituals now signify and stand in for a general black American future-past. Du Bois (re)defines the spirituals he employs by fusing them with Western canonical literature, rendering these songs usable and audible African American future-pasts that bridge the gap between the nineteenth century—slavery and white transcribers—and the twentieth century—the color line. Thus, the "Sorrow Songs" are severed from their origins by transmogrifying them into grooves for Du Bois's dub mix, which allows *Souls* to be audible and legible as the first literary sound recording (phono-graph) of sonic Afro-modernity.[1]

1. I define *sonic Afro-modernity* in relation to the advent of technological sound recording at the end of the nineteenth century (embodied in the phonograph) that offered the ability to split sounds from the sources that (re)produced them, creating a technological orality and musicality in twentieth-century black culture. In other words, oralities and musicalities were no longer tied to the immediate presence of human subjects; they became technologically iterable in a Derridean sense that occasions not so much a complete disappearance of the human subject but its resounding through new styles of technological folding. On the one hand, this disjuncture between sound and source rendered the former more ephemeral since it failed to provide the listener with a clear visual point of reference. On the other hand, sound gained its materiality in the technological apparatuses

In order to contextualize my argument about the temporalities of "sonic Afro-modernity" in Du Bois's use of the "Sorrow Songs," I turn to Ralph Ellison's *Invisible Man* ([1952] 1995) and to Walter Benjamin's "Theses on the Philosophy of History" (1969) as conceptual echo chambers. In Ellison's novel, history appears as a groove that indexes both the serrations found on the surface of phonograph records and those somewhat more elusive grooves in the vernacular sense of the term, while Benjamin imagines history as an uneven chain of monadic shrapnel that disjoins the putative continuum of empty, homogeneous time. Moreover, all three writers hone in on variable temporalities from the vantage point of the tradition of the oppressed, to use Benjamin's phrase, and consequently recalibrate the flows between the major and the minor, the future and the past. By reading these writings across time and space, my strategy quite intentionally goes against the grain of current historicist discourses in the U.S. academy, where "history" appears as commonsensical and determining in the last instance—if not necessarily progressive in a teleological sense. This often unarticulated and undertheorized account of historical time leaves intact a fairly staid configuration of temporal movement (if it includes motion at all) that cannot account for the discontinuities of the temporal in the work of Du Bois, Ellison, and Benjamin.

The Grooves of History

Chapter 20 of Ellison's *Invisible Man* suggests a notion of temporality steeped in sound technology that, thankfully, steers clear of a linear model of history. This chapter, which overflows with references to records and grooves, opens with the protagonist's search for the missing Tod Clifton, a fellow member of "The Brotherhood," a political organization. In his quest to find Clifton, the protagonist is led to Harlem where "the uptown rhythms were slower and yet somehow faster" than the ones downtown, already indicating a shift in time that will acquire more force as the protagonist's journey continues (Ellison [1952] 1995: 423). The protagonist finally locates Clifton selling "Sambo Dolls" on Forty-third Street. Clifton and his partner accompany their sales pitch with a song about the features of this doll. Comparing Clifton's activities in The Brotherhood with his new role as a Sambo Doll salesman, the protagonist ponders Clifton's fate: "It was as though he had

---

and the practices surrounding these devices and in the process rematerialized the human source. This interplay between the ephemerality of music (or the apparatus) and the materiality of the audio technologies/practices (or music) provides the central, nonsublatable tension at the core of sonic Afro-modernity. For a different consideration of Afro-modern time, see Hanchard 1999.

chosen . . . to fall outside of *history*" (Ellison [1952] 1995: 434; emphasis his). The assertion queries a commonsense approach to history; for how, if history is defined as an autonomous motor that keeps the world running, can Clifton fall out of it? What history does Clifton fall out of when he sells Sambo Dolls rather than participating in The Brotherhood? Here the protagonist seems to embody the historicist impulse by virtue of his failure to question the timeline fed to him by The Brotherhood, by accepting that there can be only a totalizing historical machine that controls the past, present, and future.

Undoubtedly, this query acquires different shades of signification for "the tradition of the oppressed." Two incidents in particular shape the protagonist's movement from—in Walter Benjamin's terminology—a historicist worldview to a historical materialist one: when he witnesses Clifton's death and when he encounters three young black men wearing zoot suits.[2] While selling the dolls, Clifton is threatened by and attacks a white policeman—a confrontation that culminates in Clifton's fatal shooting, which the protagonist unwillingly observes. Forced to bear witness to his friend's violent erasure from history—any history—the protagonist is swept up in a current of doubt, igniting a different historical motor: "Why should a man deliberately plunge outside history and peddle in obscenity? Why did he choose to plunge . . . into the void of faceless faces, of soundless voices, lying outside of history?" (Ellison [1952] 1995: 439). Clifton's death forces the protagonist to acknowledge that Clifton had no choice in "falling out of history" since there exists no place for black subjects in The Brotherhood's version of history. In this sense they are already belated, "men out of time," in Ellison's words ([1952] 1995: 441). Here, the teleological model of history ruptures; in its place, a more nuanced theory of temporality materializes that takes notice of the complex relations of domination and subordination linked to the inscription of history as it pertains to black people in the United States and the global oppressed. In this configuration, written records, and historical narratives in particular, are wrested from the sphere of totality and self-evident truth as they fail or violently resist inscribing the histories of marginalized subjects such as Clifton.

After leaving the scene of Clifton's death, the protagonist descends into the nearest subway station, where he stumbles upon three young black men dressed in zoot suits. Briefly reasserting his totalizing conceptualization of history in the aftermath of Clifton's murder, he describes them as: "Men out of time—unless they found Brotherhood. Men out of time, who would soon be gone and forgotten" (Ellison [1952] 1995: 441). Here, the zoot-suiters are beyond the measure of

2. For discussions of the culture of zoot suits, see Cossgrove 1984 and Kelley 1994.

temporality per se due to their distance from The Brotherhood; the protagonist, nevertheless, envisions this specific redaction of history qua History, eliding the differences between the particular and the universal. Paralleling the advent of Clifton's death, this encounter inspires a puncture in the seamless suture between the lowercase and uppercase types of history:

> What if history was a gambler, instead of a force in a laboratory experiment, and his boys the ace in the hole? What if history was not a reasonable citizen, but a madman full of paranoid guile and these boys his agents, his big surprise! His own revenge? For they were outside, in the dark with Sambo, the dancing paper doll; taking it on the lambo with my fallen brother, Tod Clifton (Tod, Tod) running and dodging the forces of history instead of making a dominating stand. (Ellison [1952] 1995: 441)[3]

This set of questions and the final assertion serve to further elucidate the dislocation, if not negation, of the protagonist's model of history by interrogating the role of history in relation to American culture generally and black subjects in particular. If history were a madman and not a scientific motor, would Clifton still be alive? Once history ceases to bear the semblance of a "reasonable citizen," it visibly falls short as the sign and logos of temporal convergence—a site of failure from which the protagonist can yet gain perspective on his own alienation from this machine. While the totalizing idea of the historical does not quite vanish from the horizon, it does begin to fade slightly, making room for alternatives that allocate a place ("his agents") for the zoot-suiters in a way that the former cannot. Even though Clifton and the zoot-suiters are already "recorded out" of dominant historiography, they may be partially responsible for this positioning, according to the protagonist, for they do not attempt to alter its route. This recourse to self-determination underscores the protagonist's continuing belief in The Brotherhood's unilateral notion of history, like a transcendental locomotive that Clifton and the young men can either board or let pass by. To completely, or at least principally, abandon this train of thought regarding temporality and black subjects' status in it, the protagonist will have to tune his ears to the refrain of phonograph records for a dissimilar transaction of this vexed conundrum.

Walking the streets of Harlem, the protagonist asserts: "They were *outside the groove of history*, and it was my job to get them in, all of them. Forgotten names sang through my head like forgotten scenes in dreams" (Ellison [1952] 1995: 443;

---

3. *Nomen est omen. Tod* means death in German; inscribing Tod's demise in his proper name, and its repetition in the passage cited above, would sonorically signify his overdetermined finitude.

emphasis mine). Unable to relinquish the dominant model of history propagated by The Brotherhood, which can only conceive of the zoot-suiters as embodying CPT, the protagonist imagines history as a single groove from which these men are barred even as they opt for remaining beyond its borders, thus suggesting a syncopated equilibrium between determining structure and human agency.[4] As he continues his not so leisurely stroll, however, the sonic ecology intrudes even more forcefully into the protagonist's historical shield: "I moved with the crowd, the sweat pouring off me, listening to the grinding roar of traffic, the growing sound of a record shop loudspeaker blaring a languid blues. I stopped. *Was this all that would be recorded? Was this the only true history of the times*, a mood blared by trumpets, trombones, saxophones and drums, a song with turgid, inadequate words?" (Ellison [1952] 1995: 443; emphasis mine). What distinguishes these sounds from the epochal totality promulgated by The Brotherhood is not only its imagining of an alternative historical sphere but also, and more important, the appearance of a sonic aperture that shifts the rules of the game altogether.

In what amounts to no less than an instance of a linguistic cum historical sublime, the clarity of traditional historiography is momentarily displaced by the "blaring of a loudspeaker" transmitting a variety of instruments and "turgid, inadequate words." The loudspeaker shocks the protagonist into a realm beyond the reach of linguistic signification (inadequate and turgid), wherein aggregations of phonemes cease to function as the sole determinants in the gamble of time, since they fall short of discharging the interlocking and clashing folds of temporal confluence. Put simply, the brand of history the protagonist has been hitherto accustomed to in his association with The Brotherhood can redact only one mode of historical change, leaving by the wayside those events too promiscuous to fit its teleological sequence of events. This has particular ramifications for subjects who have access to neither historiographical nor graphematic technologies (most markedly black people in the United States). Nonetheless, the written annals of history are not simply exchanged for a more authentic Afro-diasporic oral theory of history; rather, Ellison insists on the iterability of sound recording and reproduction and thus refuses to disentangle the *phono* from the *graph*, and vice versa, amounting to an additive code as opposed to an either/or proposition. But before we get ahead of ourselves, we should lend an ear to another sage voice sounding from a different virtual loudspeaker.

The protagonist's reconceptualization of the temporal suggests an instance

4. Ellison ([1952] 1995: 163) references CPT in an earlier part of the novel: "If you made an appointment, you couldn't bring them any slow c.p. (colored people's) time."

of peril (Clifton's violent demise) in which the past flares up as a monad. Such reconfigurations were underscored by Walter Benjamin, whose understanding of history opens a different series of doorways to the crinkle of the past, suggesting a nondogmatic and elastic constellation of temporal convergence rather than "the swift and imperceptible flowing of time" (Ellison [1952] 1995: 8). In his oft-cited essay, "Theses on the Philosophy of History," Benjamin (1969: 257) distinguishes between historicism, which slavishly attempts to re-create the "true past," and a historical materialism that "brush[es] history against the grain."[5] Benjamin's historical imaginary, rather than seeking to construe the past "the way it really was," aspires to "seize hold of a memory as it flashes up at a moment of danger" (Benjamin 1969: 255). As Benjamin (1969: 257) argues in a different thesis: "The tradition of the oppressed teaches us that 'the state of exception' in which we live is the rule." In this way, the historical materialist is always confronted by peril, which is precisely what puts into motion the necessity of "brushing history against the grain." But what does this brushing against yield that a cross section does not or cannot?

While the historicist accumulates facts in order to fill the dustbin of "homogeneous and empty time" that "culminates in universal history," the historical materialist works under the auspices of a "constructive principle" that incorporates its own theoretical production—he reflects on the process of assembling history as opposed to simply retelling the past—and "only approaches a historical entity where it confronts him in the form of a monad" (Benjamin 1969: 262–63). This monad appears as a breach, a wounding, as Hortense Spillers (1987) might say, in the ostensibly inevitable progressive workings of historical time and gives way to a model of "messianic time" that eschews a linear current in favor of a "cessation of happening" (Benjamin 1969: 263). The historical materialist faces—and therefore inevitably constructs—history as a secularized version of messianic temporality in which the past is released from its mimeticist straightjacket and reinvented as "a configuration of the present (*Jetztzeit*) which is shot through with shrapnel of the messianic" (Benjamin 1969: 263). The shards of messianism enable a revision not only of the historical, but of temporality as such, forming hiccups in the machine of "universal history," hiccups which do not suspend or dispense with this (chrono)logical mode so much as they provide pathways to the clefts and folds within its very configurations. In Edouard Glissant's terminology (1997: 145): the (weak) messianic imagines temporality as series of opacities, while historicism only apprehends the past, present, and future as silenced by the

5. I have altered the translation of Benjamin's text where necessary.

screech of clarity. These weak messianics conjure a different form of temporal materiality, in which the material is syncopated in a constant flux rather than held in the abyss of universal time. In an attempt to perforate "the swift and imperceptible flowing of time," Ellison, much like Benjamin, tenders an arrangement of temporal change that bypasses quasi-positivist ideas concerning history, especially with regard to "the tradition of the oppressed."

Ellison's insistence on the sonic's traversal of the phonograph proves decisive, as it recalibrates not only temporality but also the function of *graph* in historiography rather than claiming for black cultural purposes an authentic orality uncontaminated by the modern technological viruses. Hence, Ellison's "hero" comes upon Benjamin's flash in a moment of danger—Clifton's death—via the electric amplification of a phonograph record and not, to put it bluntly, a "real" live singer or musician. Clearly, blackness and alterity in general are inscribed in and sound from the sonorous fissure of the "grooves of history." These grooves, in turn, serve a double purpose: they displace—once again, it is necessary to insist that they do not replace—a historicist model of time; but they also sharply suggest how in the processes of sound recording and reproduction, the production of black history transmogrifies from absolute erasure in writing to sounding from loudspeakers on any given urban corner. And these amplifiers echo not only "turgid and inadequate words," but also predominantly nonlinguistic sonic marks. In this way, black subjects are not intrinsically outside of history, as G. W. F. Hegel would have it a century before Ellison, but are actively and often ferociously "recorded out" of it, which, in turn, has led to the forging of other means to record black history. In the Ellisonian cosmos, these instruments appear in, through, and with the phonographic sounds because of, and not despite, the iterability the machine introduces into the realm of black aurality. In other words, the repetition thrown into the whirlpool of transversal movement by this particular technicity of black music in the age of mechanical reproduction—that here should not be equated with technicity per se but with a new form of technological folding—enables a fresh recording and sounding of black history. Neither an authentic black orality nor a thoroughly commodified and inauthentic version thereof suffices to stage black history qua history; instead, we are confronted with a sounding black history that hinges on mechanical and electrical iterability, suggesting a different form of writing than the fraught domain of alphabetic script and one that makes black sounds mechanically repeatable.

If we return to the most common senses of *groove*, we can better surmise how history might operate as one. First, the term refers to the serrations on the surface of phonograph records or any indentation; and second, we find it in colloquial expressions, such as "the groove" of a particular piece of music or "getting into the groove" of someone or something. Both these senses of groove are derived from musical expressions, if not directly related to the sonic. While the grooves on records present a seemingly straightforward traffic between word and object, the other signification of groove proves slightly more intangible if not elusive (a more Du Boisian and Derridean signifier/signified relationship than a Saussurean one); for instance, there are no objective ways to describe or pin down the groove of a James Brown track. This does not connote incoherence, but it does highlight the difficulty in transfiguring the exact characteristics of the groove into the realm of linguistic meaning making: the groove contains a significant measure of opacity because it registers in the domain of affect and sensation rather than (linguistic) signification. For Steven Feld and Charles Keil, this can be attributed to the "collaborative expectancies in time" that lead to an agreement between musicians and their audiences that unites them in an open-ended and unevenly striated rapport, thus amplifying the nonrepresentational aspects of sound.[6] These "expectancies in time" are also mediated, if not constituted, by the grooves of phonograph records; they provide the material groundings for intersubjective grooves.

The "groove of history" allows for both the materiality and the intersubjectivity of history; if black history is indeed contained on, or at least summoned by, phonograph records, it is only because the discs and their attendant discourses and practices harbor all these vital forces. Ellison's protagonist comes upon this recognition in an instance of peril, which provokes his recognition of temporality as a series of monadic crosscurrents and discontinuities as opposed to a single and totalizing history. These relational grooves, however, cannot be consigned to the realm of the purely subjective, since they direct our awareness to dimensions of temporality that are not signified by the strictures of written history or even the indentations on phonograph records alone. Therefore, both forms of grooves—at least in the universe of recorded music—are not only mutually constitutive but bring each other into productive crisis. The groove of history works well in this regard because it fails to neglect one aspect in favor of the other; instead it preserves, or possibly invents, the eventness of temporality as sonically singular. Still, should we not ask what transpires when different grooves of history interface or collide? W. E. B. Du Bois's *The Souls of Black Folk* will

6. Feld and Keil (1994: 109) describe the colloquial dimension of groove in the following fashion: "In the vernacular a 'groove' refers to an intuitive sense of style as process, a perception of a cycle in motion, a form or organizing pattern being revealed, a recurrent clustering of elements through time. Groove and style are distilled essences, crystallizations of collaborative expectancies in time."

serve as our sonorous guide on this journey back and forth through the assorted time(s) of sonic Afro-modernity.

Phono-Epi-Graphs

In his analysis of the different functions of spirituals in nineteenth-century and early-twentieth-century American culture, Ronald Radano (1996: 508) begins by charting the white fascination with spirituals after they had been transcribed during the Civil War, arguing that spirituals represented "the outer limits of the western imagination." This was integrally tied to the conundrum of transcription; most whites "writing down" the spirituals noted the difficulties in "capturing" these on paper.[7] In the minds of northern white abolitionists, spirituals became a part of a larger romantic ideology that believed music could counter Western reason as an anticivilizational prophylactic, especially since certain strands of romanticism in general were obsessed with replacing reason, the central concept of the enlightenment, with "untainted" and "natural" cultural productions that led man back to his original state. Romanticist thinkers, due in part to increased interest in folk culture, argued that these apparently natural and authentic cultural forms possessed qualities lacking in "spoiled" high-cultural production. As musical ruminations of folk culture, spirituals were doubly coded as authentic artifacts that provided a true representation of black humanity. Jon Cruz (1999: 5) extends Radano's important argument by showing how spirituals formed a fundamental component not only of romanticist qua abolitionist conversations but also of burgeoning social scientific discourses (ethnomusicology and anthropology, in particular) and how, in Cruz's formulation, "romantic antimodernism and rational social science converge and intersect in the discovery of the Negro spiritual." The combined force of these two divergent figurations of discourse, and therefore of blackness, projected the spirituals as the "preferred black culture" for both white and black commentators from the mid–nineteenth century on (Cruz 1999: 7).[8] In

7. Writing down acquires a particular resonance in relation to the German title of Friedrich Kittler's *Discourse Networks 1800/1900* (*Aufschreibsysteme 1800/1900*). David Wellbery, in his introduction to the English translation of this work (Kittler: 1990: xii), shows that the title "can be most literally translated as 'systems of writing down' or 'notation systems.' It refers to a level of material deployment that is prior to questions of meaning. . . . In Kittler's view, such technologies are not mere instruments with which 'man' produces his meanings, . . . rather they set the framework within which something like 'meaning,' indeed, something like 'man,' becomes possible at all."

8. Cruz (1999: 164–88) interrogates the importance of spirituals to the formation of African American institutions of higher learning. Clearly the Fisk Jubilee Singers represent a crucial part of this assemblage.

this context, musical notation served to amplify both the primitive unrepresent-
ability *and* the rationalization of spirituals, which is rendered even more overdetermined if we take into account, as Radano does, how the process of transcribing
spirituals forced some scribes to thoroughly recast the Western system of musical
notation. As a consequence, the notations that appear in Du Bois's text are already
notations in difference, differential notes, originary remixes, or, as Fred Moten
(2003: 14) has argued, "an ongoing event of antiorigin and an antiorigin, replay
and reverb of an impossible natal occasion, the performance of a birth and rebirth
of a new science, a phylogenetic fantasy that (dis)establishes genesis, the reproduction of blackness as (the) reproduction of black performance(s)." Not only
does the presence of the fragments of musical bars alter the text of *Souls*, but the
notation itself has been transformed into another "writing down system" by virtue
of its encoding spirituals rather than Western classical music, transacting on a different scale black culture's constitutive part in Western modernity.

Du Bois's use of spirituals calls into question their representability in the Western system of musical notation while pointing to the limits of the method itself. As
a result, the spirituals mirror Du Bois's own double textual strategy, which mixes
"major" and "minor" cultural archives as opposed to merely using one to mimic
the other. The musical notes, like the entire text, form a mix that transforms two
distinct parts into a temporary fusion that highlights its own impurity.[9] Moreover,
Du Bois heightens the fragmentation of the spirituals by inserting musical bars
and only the beginning of each song into the text, thus rendering it even more
unlikely that readers actually recognize them. In fact, that the spirituals would
have been readable only to those who both knew the songs *and* could crack their
notation gives rise to a certain disjuncture between *Souls* and its audiences, one
that transforms the bars of the spirituals before each chapter into "mute ciphers"
that call attention to their own failure to represent sound (Gibson 1989: xvi).
As we have established, the "Sorrow Songs" cannot sonically represent a true
and authentic African American past, for the media (written collections) through
which they were transmitted had been transformed into something altogether
different prior to their Du Boisian figuration. This alteration shapes the spirituals into future-oriented artifacts that sound an opaque and fragmented African
American past. Consequently, the temporality suggested by Du Bois's textual
strategies resemble Ellison's "grooves" and Benjamin's "monadic shrapnel" rather
than any movement that would fit into a historicist notion of history; they render

9. For the most convincing and influential account of syncretism in slave culture in general and
spirituals in particular, see Levine 1977.

the spirituals as grooves in Du Bois's own textual collage. Surely, the sedimented meanings ascribed to and inscribed in these marks puncture the Du Boisian text, though they are significantly re-sounded as well.

Overall, what is at stake in Du Bois's transcription is not whether these spirituals can find an adequate written home that represents them faithfully but what their fragmentary status does to the text of *Souls*. The "Sorrow Songs" suggest a Freudian *unheimlich* (uncanny)—as opposed to homeliness in any traditional sense—as they intimate quasi-indecipherable musical signs that disrupt the flow of words and add to the texturality of the text (Freud 2003). Situated at the interstices of text (lyrical epigraphs) and words (chapters), these sonorous residues implode the linguistic utterances that frame them. While the musical epigraphs haunt the full text of *Souls* by way of suggestion, they stand on their own as booming, yet mute, phono-epi-graphs at the intersection of the poems and the body of the text. Rather than serving as mere afterthoughts, they radically alter the significations of the text via their constitutive supplementarity.

Du Bois continues the transformation of spirituals initiated by their improvisatory beginnings and subsequent transcription by fusing them with poems from the nineteenth-century European canon. The flow between the musical bars of the spirituals and mostly nineteenth-century British poems in *Souls* is the clearest example of Du Bois's mixology. Here I am not so much concerned with how the musical epigraphs interact with Du Bois's writing as I am with the sonic signifiers' refiguration of the poems that they trail. Far too often critics have assumed a certain stability to the poems' significations, though even as their placement in a literary context alters the spirituals, it also fundamentally transforms the poems, dislodging them from their enshrined canonicity. Thus Arthur Symons's poem, which opens the first chapter, becomes legible as a lament against chattel slavery and a testimony to the "Spiritual Strivings" of black subjects:

> Unresting water, there shall never be rest
> till the last moon droop and the last tide fail,
> And *the fire of the end begin to burn in the west*;
> And the heart shall be weary and wonder and cry like the sea,
> All life long crying without avail,
> As the water all night long is crying to me.
> (Symons in Du Bois [1903] 1989: 3; emphasis mine)

Once attuned to Du Bois's mixing maneuvers, they appear as another manifestation of the spirituals—Du Bois's incorporation releases the poems' Afro-entelechy. Initially, what is most striking is the existential despair of these words that eerily

echoes many of the "Sorrow Songs," particularly "Nobody Knows the Trouble I
Have Seen," which is paired with the Symons poem. The chorus of this spiritual
reads as follows:

> Oh, nobody knows the trouble I've seen,
> Nobody knows but Jesus,
> Nobody knows the trouble I've seen,
> Glory Hallelujah.

The poem and the lyrics of the spiritual suggest troubles and plagued souls, yet
in both instances the reasons for these woes are not disclosed. Clearly, Du Bois
takes advantage of this poetic haziness in order to make the words applicable to
the souls of black folk, and in this way, the "weariness" and "crying" articulated
by the speaker become testimonies of and to *Souls*'s collective black voice. And
read in the mixological milieu of *Souls*, the line from Symons's poem, "the fire of
the end begin to burn in the west," offers a pertinent observation concerning the
role of race in Western modernity—so central to Du Bois's argument. According
to this eschatology, the apocalypse will not be precipitated by biblical sins, at
least not in any strict sense, but by the secular crimes of the West (the specters
of slavery, racism, and imperialism). Where earlier African American discourses
(in spirituals, poetry, slave narratives, or spiritual narratives) coded secular prob-
lematics in religious language, Du Bois ([1903] 1989: 13) interfaces the spirituals
and the poems to launch a decidedly this-worldly critique of Western modernity:
"the problem of the twentieth century is the problem of the color-line—the relation of the darker to the lighter races of the men in Asia and Africa, in America
and the islands of the sea." Du Bois does not merely quote, at least not in any
simple fashion, Symons's poem. By meshing its beat with the syncopated styl-
ings of "Nobody Knows" and his own words in "Of Our Spiritual Strivings," he
gives it a new signification that is legible and audible exclusively in *Souls*. This
splintered synthesis of Western canonical literature and black musical expression
inaugurates all of *Souls*'s chapters, save the last, which combines the music from
one spiritual with the lyrics of another.

If Du Bois transposes spirituals into the realm of "legitimate" written culture, he vernacularizes European writing. A similar strategy will be later used
by many black musicians, most famously in John Coltrane's rendition of "My
Favorite Things" or DJs' remixes of previously recorded grooves. Poems by
Schiller, Byron, Lowell, and Whittier thus form a symbiosis with the spirituals.
Du Bois slyly forces these Western texts to testify to slavery and the absent presence of black subjects, both as empirical entities and as apparitions integral *to*

and unequivocally *of* Western modernity. Read or listened to in tandem with the musical bars, then, the poems *are* the lyrics to the "Sorrow Songs," creating a new form of spiritual in their admixture. All of these layers in Du Bois's textual mixology exemplify the aesthetic complexity and cultural flexibility of sonic (black) temporality. And this sonic-textual temporality does not simply reverse the order of things but generates a genuinely new modality, a different groove, inimitable in its insistence on and performance of the coevalness of the "Sorrow Songs" and the annals of literary canonicity. Johannes Fabian (1983: 143) has shown that the central discourse of anthropology resolutely denies the temporal equality of the Western other (generally the primitive or some reformulation thereof), choosing instead to "establish itself as an allochronic discourse; it is the science of other men in another Time." Du Bois's style of coevalness exhumes the internal crises in the still-warm corpses of reason and progress even while it constructs a different time in which reason and terror, progress and regress coexist in a momentary détente. Nowhere is this more apparent than in the phono-epi-graphic mix placed before the final chapter of *Souls*.

In the final chapter of *Souls*, Du Bois presents a theory of the "Sorrow Songs," discussing their aesthetic, cultural, and political dimensions in addition to providing an autohistorical account of how African songs transmuted into spirituals in the aftermath of the Middle Passage. The chapter's two epigraphs fail to comply with the scheme Du Bois has thus far established: both the lyrical and musical headings are drawn from the reservoir of the "Sorrow Songs," in contrast to the previous chapters, which are introduced by one musical and one poetic epigraph. At first glance, this might imply that "The Sorrow Songs" establishes some sort of unity, in terms of both structure and content, in ways that the remaining chapters do not, a unity that in turn harks back to mechanisms of double consciousness: the black sonic marks (i.e., the words to a spiritual) erase and replace white words (the epigraphic poems), giving the structural feature of a page back its originary stature as black and white recede to their preordained places in the universe. Nonetheless, for all intents and purposes, there is no end of history in *Souls*—maybe an eternal return, but no closure in sight or sound. The two epigraphs preceding "The Sorrow Songs" implement rupture within this field of presumed unity given that they do not stem from the same spiritual: the lyrics are from "Lay This Body Down," while the musical notes are those of "Wrestling Jacob." By juxtaposing two different spirituals, Du Bois defies any easy dichotomy between black and white or major and minor. In the end, merging the music of one spiritual with the lyrics of another projects a new spiritual that encodes the multitude of significations the "Sorrow Songs" had acquired in 1903 but also, and perhaps more significantly, makes them future-compatible. In this final twinning, the past, present, and future coexist to generate the temporal grooves of sonic Afro-modernity.

Overall, Du Bois suffuses *Souls* with the "non-wordness" of sounds—the aspects of sound that cannot be reproduced on the written page, or in Du Bois's formulation ([1903] 1989: 207), which is echoed by Ellison's, "turgid and inadequate words," "knowing as little as our fathers what its words may mean, but knowing well the meaning of its music." Du Bois's attempt to provide written words with a sonorous surplus structures *Souls* as a phono-graph that attempts to make the souls of black folk *sound* and *be heard*. This not through a strict opposition between notated sounds and written words but through an augmentation of words with sounds, by adding back into the mix what gets left out in the equation of language and speech with linguistic structures. Du Bois indexes the "Sorrow Songs" he intends to use as epigraphs, stating that "some echo of haunting melody" will appear in his text, insinuating that their melodies—which are not the most important aspect of spirituals anyway—can be recorded by Du Bois and deciphered by the readers only as figural excess. The readers become privy to the titles of the spirituals used as epigraphs in the final chapter, yet even there Du Bois does not disclose the spirituals contained in the spectral assemblage of *Souls*, nor does he clarify where the individual song is placed in the text. This reticence, and the confusion it creates, exemplifies the distorted reverberations of black sounds, since the spirituals that Du Bois cites appear in the text not as accurate representations but as distorted, layered, and lingering traces. Through these melodic fragments, the voices of the slaves that composed, sang, and improvised upon these songs uncannily haunt the textual house of *Souls*. No one-to-one likeness of these songs will accomplish Du Bois's goal, hence his invocation is an echoing rather than a mimetic technique.

Using Du Bois's terminology, we can imagine *Souls* as an extended echo chamber in which traces of the spirituals reverberate with and against one other, forming a textuo-sonic machine that differs from the previously available compilations of spirituals. This becomes significant vis-à-vis *Souls* if we consider that most of its essays were previously published, recombined, and augmented for their appearance in *Souls*. Du Bois remixes his own words or rather, as we shall see, engineers a "dub version" of his own texts and the "Sorrow Songs."[10] In this way, *Souls*

---

10. Robert Stepto has already analyzed the significations of the changes with regard to form as well as content. Stepto (1979: 53–59) attributes the majority of the shifts and resignifications in *Souls* to Du Bois's reaction to Booker T. Washington. For the purposes of my argument, it suffices to note that this adds yet another layer to the mix as it manifests itself in Du Bois's text.

reverberates dialogically with one of the most significant Afro-diasporic aesthetic achievements of the past fifty years: dub reggae, without which most contemporary popular music would simply not exist. In the late sixties, Jamaican producers started messing with the musical text via technological means: loosening its confines, turning up the bass and drum in the mix, distorting and displacing the centrality of the voice, opening it up to the cosmos. These aesthetic formations have cast a midday shadow—much in the same way Du Bois has in the annals of American literary and political discourses—over much of popular music since then, including disco, hip-hop, and contemporary electronic dance music. As Bill Brewster and Frank Broughton (1999: 119) explain, "A dub mix is essentially the bare bones of a track with bass turned up. Dub separates a song into its stark component parts, and adds and subtracts each strand until a new composition is made. By adding space to the track, what is left has far more room to breathe."[11] A couple of points remain salient in the resonance between *Souls* and dub's Afro-tricknology: the style with which Du Bois recasts the spirituals via the technology of musical notation and his invocation of echo and haunting in the text. Echo, with reverb and delay, remains one of dub's core features, inserting spatiality into the musical track while also messing with its temporal dimensions; in fact, the spatial effect of echo is achieved via the stuttering and dispersion of the music's time. The term *dub* itself indicates not only a doubling or copying but carries homonymic overtones of *duppy* (the Jamaican word for "spirit" or "ghost"), so that the dub version of a song serves as a spectral other that was initially pressed on the flip side of its record, even as it often became far more popular than its source. In this echo box, Freud's theory of the uncanny, especially as it passes through the doppelgänger, coexists with Du Bois's notion of doubling and spectrality and returns to us from the margins of the contemporary African diaspora in an altered sonic form: dub, duppy, double consciousness, and the uncanny unveil the haunting at the center of the "real," which according to Avery Gordon (1997: 8), "is a very particular way of knowing what has happened or is happening . . . as transformative recognition." This "particular way of knowing" that moves with spirits

11. In *Reggae: The Rough Guide*, Steve Barrow and Peter Dalton (1997: 199) offer the following concise redaction of dub reggae's three main historical stages and movement from margin to center: "First there was the so-called 'instrumentals,' not originally conceived as such, but becoming so by removal of the vocal track. Initially these instrumentals were strictly for sound-system play, but before too long they were being issued commercially. Versions on which the contribution of the studio engineer was more obvious then emerged around the end of 1968, and by 1970 these remixes—called 'versions'—were appearing on B-sides of most Jamaican singles. . . . During 1973–74 record buyers in Jamaica became accustomed to checking labels not just for the producer or artist, but also for the engineer."

as integral to the totality of social life worlds finds its textual-sonic correlative in *Souls*'s figuration of the "Sorrow Songs," since rather than being auxiliary, their spectral absent presence enables the signification of the Du Boisian text, both in terms of thematics and structure. Thus, the *Geist*—what Du Bois ([1903] 1989: 204) terms "the gift of Spirit"—of dub/*duppy* allows us to think haunting as echo and vice versa, excavating the sonorous facets of this spectral ontology at the limit of empirical knowledge and livability. Hearing voices will never quite be the same again; for what comprises an echo, always a multiplicity of one (the one?), if not the clashing reverberations of a dead sound that lives in its aftereffects and therefore resists finitude, even as mortality forms the core of its spirit?

Benjamin, like Ellison and Du Bois, was also attuned to the lower sonic cum spectral frequencies of the past, writing: "Streift uns nicht selber ein Hauch der Luft, die um die Früheren gewesen ist? Ist nicht in Stimmen, denen wir unser Ohr schenken ein Echo von nun verstummten?" (Doesn't a breath of air around our predecessors graze us? Is not, in the voices we lend our ears to, an echo of the now muted?) (Benjamin 1980: 251).[12] I reproduce the German here because these two sentences were omitted from the English translation in *Illuminations* (1969), the compilation that precipitated Benjamin's popularization in the Anglo-American academy and beyond and that contained, until recently, the only English translation of Benjamin's essay. The voices of the dead spectrally infuse Benjamin's discourse, adding a sonic dimension to his monadic conception of the historical. In a number of ways they also remember, repeat, and work through Du Bois's plea that his readers hear the souls of black folk and his insistence that only "an echo of haunting melody" can materialize in the text. Moreover, these lines' exclusion from the translation and their concern with sound amplify both the volume of this echo and the spectrality of temporality; they only exist in the ghostly shadow of Benjamin's text. Thus, *The Souls of Black Folk* transacts the confluence of differing and differential grooves that add up to a dub mix, a sonic hauntology of the temporal in which both the past and the future echo in the present, only to transform its status as presence.[13]

12. Translation mine. These sentences have been included in the recent translation as part of the fourth volume of Benjamin's *Selected Writings* (2003).

13. The field of thought opened by Du Bois and Benjamin concerning echo, haunting, and temporality also makes several appearances in Deleuze's theater of *Difference and Repetition*. Therein, moving through the groundwork of Nietzsche and Kierkegaard, Deleuze stages repetition as a series of anti-/nonrepresentational singularities. At several key moments in the argument, Deleuze (1994: 1) makes echo a major player in this drama, for instance: "Reflections, echoes, doubles, and souls do not belong to the domain of resemblance and equivalence." While I have been influenced by Deleuze's idea of repetition throughout this essay, here I want to draw the reader's attention to "souls" and "echoes" as instantiations of the singular in Du Bois and Deleuze.

If Ellison and Benjamin detonate grooves and monadic shrapnel within the province of the historicist past, Du Bois performs this temporal explosion, where different flows, velocities, and grooves collide through the structural mixology of *Souls*'s epigraphs, particularly the final one. In other words, Ellison and Benjamin offer the tools for conjecturing nonhistoricist compilations of the temporal a propos the tradition of the oppressed and the sonic. That *The Souls of Black Folk* enacts these principles structurally ought not involve any sort of rift between the theoretical and the performative, in contrast to sundry manifestations of analogous principles vis-à-vis temporality in different modes of discursive materiality. And while these imaginings of time are drawn from those oppressed subjects behind the veil and outside the groove of history, we should not be so quick to relegate these imperative contributions to twentieth-century intellectual and cultural history to an already established minoritarian status. Instead, we might do well to think how these formations remix the temporality of modernity per se. Du Bois, Ellison, and Benjamin ratify, reimagine, and morselize the supposed linearity of hegemonic time from the (aural) vantage point of the oppressed.

Overall, it is sound that allows these diverse laborers in the kingdom of culture to mess with the strict cadence of Western modernity in order to present us with a disjointed and singular sonic Afro-modernity, giving credence to Gilles Deleuze and Félix Guattari's observation (1987: 313) that "meter is dogmatic, but rhythm critical." These writings or practices rhythmify temporality via syncopation, taking on variously the form of grooves, monadic shrapnel, and haunting echoes of the past, present, and future. Time ceases to behave solely as meter only when these three forces coexist, even if unequally and in a fragmented manner, and their contemporaneousness is aided by their proximity to the margins of Western modernity. In a recently unearthed essay about the vicissitudes of positivism in U.S. social scientific discourse at the turn of the last century, Du Bois (2000: 44) uses rhythm to delineate the grounds of empirical knowability: "a primary rhythm depending . . . on physical forces and physical law; but within it appears again and again a secondary rhythm, which while presenting nearly the same uniformity as the first, differs from it in its more or less sudden rise at a given tune." In conclusion, we can say that Ellison, Du Bois, and Benjamin insert this secondary rhythm (or *riddim*, to summon an Afro-diasporic rendition of this term) into Western modernity. Generally, this *riddim* is rendered inaudible even as it transacts the echoing strain and complementarity between these rhythms. Yet, as all of these figures show, once the latter beat, much like a ghost, is introduced to the mix, it no longer remains secondary or belated; rather it unbolts altogether new and different versions of time, synonymous with the rhythms found in and sounding from the grooves of sonic Afro-modernity.

Alexander G. Weheliye is assistant professor of English and African American studies at Northwestern University. He is the author of *Phonographies: Grooves in Sonic Afro-Modernity* (2005), from which this essay is taken.

References

Barrow, Steve, and Peter Dalton. 1997. *Reggae: The rough guide*. New York: Penguin.

Benjamin, Walter. 1969. Theses on the philosophy of history. In *Illuminations: Essays and reflections*, edited by Hannah Arendt and translated by Harry Zohn. New York: Schocken.

———. 1980. Über den Begriff der Geschichte (On the concept of history). In *Illuminationen: Ausgewählte Schriften*. Frankfurt am Main: Suhrkamp.

———. 2003. *Selected writings*. Vol. 4, *1938–1940*, translated by Edmund Jephcott et al. and edited by Howard Eiland and Michael Jennings. Cambridge, Mass.: Harvard University Press.

Brewster, Bill, and Frank Broughton. 1999. *Last night a DJ saved my life: The history of the disc jockey*. New York: Grove.

Cossgrove, Stuart. 1984. The zoot suit and style warfare. *History Workshop Journal* 18: 77–91.

Cruz, Jon. 1999. *Culture on the margins: The black spiritual and the rise of American cultural interpretation*. Princeton, N.J.: Princeton University Press.

Deleuze, Gilles. 1994. *Difference and repetition*, translated by Paul Patton. New York: Columbia University Press.

Deleuze, Gilles, and Félix Guattari. 1987. *A thousand plateaus: Capitalism and schizophrenia*, translated by Brian Massumi. Minneapolis: University of Minnesota Press.

Du Bois, W. E. B. [1903] 1989. *The souls of black folk*. New York: Penguin.

———. 2000. Sociology hesitant. *boundary 2* 27, no. 3: 37–44.

Durant, Alan. 1984. *Conditions of music*. Albany: State University of New York Press.

Ellison, Ralph. [1952] 1995. *Invisible man*. New York: Random House.

Fabian, Johannes. 1983. *Time and the other: How anthropology makes its object*. New York: Columbia University Press.

Feld, Steven, and Charles Keil. 1994. *Music grooves.* Chicago: University of Chicago Press.

Freud, Sigmund. 2003. The uncanny. In *The uncanny,* translated by David McClintock. New York: Penguin.

Gibson, Donald. 1989. Introduction. In *The souls of black folk.* New York: Penguin.

Glissant, Edouard. 1997. *Poetics of relation,* translated by Betsy Wing. Ann Arbor: University of Michigan Press.

Gordon, Avery. 1997. *Haunted matters: Haunting and the sociological imagination.* Minneapolis: University of Minnesota Press.

Hanchard, Michael. 1999. Afro-modernity: Temporality, politics, and the African diaspora. *Public Culture* 11: 245–68.

Kelley, Robin D. G. 1994. The riddle of the zoot: Malcolm Little and black cultural politics during World War II. In *Race rebels: Culture, politics, and the black working class.* New York: Free Press.

Kittler, Friedrich A. 1990. *Discourse networks 1800/1900,* translated by Michael Metteer with Chris Cullens. Stanford, Calif.: Stanford University Press.

Levine, Lawrence. 1977. *Black culture and black consciousness: Afro-American folkthought from slavery to freedom.* New York: Oxford University Press.

Moten, Fred. 2003. *In the break: The aesthetics of the black radical tradition.* Minneapolis: University of Minnesota Press.

Radano, Ronald. 1996. Denoting difference: The writing of slave spirituals. *Critical Inquiry* 22: 506–44.

Spillers, Hortense J. 1987. Mama's baby, papa's maybe: An American grammar book. *Diacritics* 17, no. 2: 65–81.

Stepto, Robert B. 1979. *From behind the veil: A study of Afro-American narrative.* Urbana: University of Illinois Press.

Sundquist, Eric. 1993. *To wake the nations: Race in the making of American literature.* Cambridge, Mass.: Harvard University Press.

See inside front cover for ordering information.

Clashing Cultures

Robert D. Aguirre

Informal Empire
Mexico and Central America in Victorian Culture

Behind the ancient artifacts exhibited in our museums lies a secret past—of travel, desire, and even theft. *Informal Empire* recaptures the history of the artifacts from Mexico and Central America that stirred Victorian interest.

"A must-read book." —Nancy Armstrong

$19.95 paper • $59.95 cloth • 296 pages

Eithne Luibhéid and Lionel Cantú Jr., editors

Queer Migrations
Sexuality, U.S. Citizenship, and Border Crossings

At the intersection of citizenship, sexuality, and race, a new perspective on the immigrant experience.

"Powerfully unpacks the ways in which state mechanisms police borders and bodies simultaneously." —Gayatri Gopinath

$19.95 paper • $59.95 cloth • 248 pages

Jill H. Casid

Sowing Empire
Landscape and Colonization

Considers imperial relandscaping and how it contributed to the construction of imperial power.

$24.95 paper • $74.95 cloth • 312 pages

Tariq Modood

Multicultural Politics
Racism, Ethnicity, and Muslims in Britain
Foreword by Craig Calhoun

Examines the modern problem of religious identity and cultural racism.

$22.95 paper • $68.95 cloth • 272 pages
Contradictions Series, volume 22

Alev Çınar

Modernity, Islam, and Secularism in Turkey
Bodies, Places, and Time

Reveals modernity as a transformative intervention in bodies, places, and times.

$19.95 paper • $59.95 cloth • 240 pages
Public Worlds Series, volume 14

University of Minnesota Press
www.upress.umn.edu • 773-702-7000

UNIVERSITY OF | PENNSYLVANIA
PRESS

THE PHILADELPHIA NEGRO
A Social Study
W. E. B. Du Bois
Introduction by Elijah Anderson
In 1897 a promising young sociologist, William Edward Burghardt Du Bois (1868–1963), was given a temporary post as Assistant in Sociology at the University of Pennsylvania in order to conduct in-depth studies of the Negro community in Philadelphia. The product of those studies was the first great empirical book on the Negro in American society.
1995 | 568 PAGES | PAPER | $17.95

THE NEGRO
W. E. B. Du Bois
Afterword by Robert Gregg
Originally published in 1915, *The Negro* is one of the first comprehensive histories of African and African-derived peoples, from their early cultures through the period of the slave trade and into the twentieth century. In his examination of race as a social construct having no foundation in biology, Du Bois anticipates much recent scholarship, and *The Negro* remains fresh, dynamic, and insightful to this day.
2001 | 288 PAGES | 4 MAPS | PAPER | $15.95

W. E. B. DU BOIS, RACE, AND THE CITY
"The Philadelphia Negro" and Its Legacy
Edited by Michael B. Katz and Thomas J. Sugrue
A group of the nation's leading historians and sociologists celebrate the centenary of his project through a reappraisal of his book. Together these essays show that *The Philadelphia Negro* remains a vital and relevant book.
1998 | 304 PAGES | 12 ILLUS. | PAPER | $19.95

THE QUEST OF THE SILVER FLEECE
A Novel
W. E. B. Du Bois
Illustrated by H. S. De Lay
Set in Alabama and Washington, D.C., in the early part of the twentieth century, Du Bois's first novel weaves the themes of racial equality and understanding through the stark reality of prejudice and bias. Originally published in 1911 and conceived immediately after *The Souls of Black Folk*, Du Bois turned to fiction to carry his message to a popular audience who were unfamiliar with his nonfiction works.
PINE STREET BOOKS
2004 | 440 PAGES | 4 ILLUS. | PAPER | $16.50

BUILDING THE NATION
Americans Write About Their Architecture, Their Cities, and Their Landscape
Edited by Steven Conn and Max Page
Through an enormous range of American voices, some famous and some obscure, and across more than two centuries of history, this anthology shows that the struggle to imagine what kinds of buildings and land use would best suit the nation pervaded all classes of Americans and was not the purview only of architects and designers. Some of the nation's finest writers, including Mark Twain, W. E. B. Du Bois, Henry James, Edith Wharton, Lewis Mumford, E. B. White, and John McPhee, are here, contemplating the American way of building.
2003 | 424 PAGES | 47 ILLUS.
CLOTH | $59.95 | PAPER | $24.95

W.E.B. DuBois

The **NEGRO**

Africans and the Diaspora

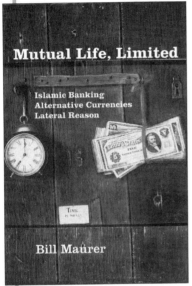

Harlan Davidson

THE PROGRESSIVE ERA AND RACE: REACTION AND REFORM, 1900–1917

DAVID W. SOUTHERN
WESTMINSTER COLLEGE

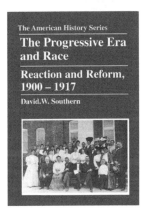

The American History Series

The Progressive Era and Race

Reaction and Reform, 1900 – 1917

David.W. Southern

This comprehensive, unflinching volume vividly portrays the ruthless exploitation, brutality, and violence inflicted on African Americans in the early twentieth century. In the South, where most blacks resided, white progressives followed racist demagogues, consolidating the Jim Crow system. In addition, southern whites liberally employed fraud, intimidation, and violence to repress blacks. Most northern progressives, meanwhile, were either indifferent to the fate of southern blacks or actively supported the social system in the South, while reformers became ensnared in a web of "scientific racism" that convinced them that blacks were inferior. Despite the adversity, African Americans courageously fought racism. The last chapter of the book reveals how the modern civil rights movement emerged—including the Niagra Movement and the rise of the NAACP—during the hostile feud between Booker T. Washington and W.E.B. Du Bois. And unlike many of the other short books on this subject, space is given to many other important African American leaders as well. **256 pages. Includes Photographs, Bibliographical Essay, and Index. Paperback, $15.95 ISBN: 0-88295-234-X © 2005**

"The strengths of this book are manifest: graceful and engaging prose; an organization that builds momentum as the narrative progresses; broad-ranging analyses of how race permeated virtually every aspect of American life; and many fascinating discussions of the changing definitions of race. . . . A moving volume that will fit well into Harlan Davidson's American History Series."

Loren Schweninger,
University of North Carolina at Greensboro

Harlan Davidson, Inc. • 773 Glenn Avenue, Wheeling, Illinois • Phone 847-541-9720 • Fax 847-541-9830 • E-mail: harlandavidson@harlandavidson.com

Visit us at www.harlandavidson.com.

RADICAL
HISTORY *Review*

Button assemblage by
Yael Simpson Fletcher
Photographed by Jean Langlois

Another World Was Possible:
A Century of Movements
Spring 2005, Issue 92

Duane J. Corpis and Ian Christopher Fletcher,
special issue editors

Another World Was Possible modifies the slogan of the World
Social Forum—an annual meeting formed as an alternative to the
more elite World Economic Forum—"Another world is possible!"
The change from present to past tense in the phrase acknowledges
the importance of social movements from the past century that
have worked for alternative visions of justice and freedom leading
up to and influencing current movements. By emphasizing social
movements and political contention, this issue offers a globalized
radical history that enriches the wider field of world history.

SUBSCRIPTION INFORMATION
Three issues annually
Institutions: $105
Individuals: $35
Students: $22 (with photocopy of valid student ID)
Single issues: $14 each
Canadian orders: Please include 7% GST and $9 postage.
Orders outside the U.S. and Canada: Please include $12 postage.

To place your order using a credit card, call 888-651-0122 (toll-free in the U.S.
and Canada) or 919-688-5134; or e-mail subscriptions@dukeupress.edu.

www.dukeupress.edu/rhr

REVIEW
FERNAND BRAUDEL CENTER

**A Journal of the
Fernand Braudel Center for the Study of
Economies, Historical Systems, and Civilizations**

Vol. XXVIII in 2005 has special issues on

The Black World and the World-System

Discussions of Knowledge

and

In Honor of Vitorino Magalhães Godinho

Previous Special Issues and Sections still available include:

XXVII, 4, 2004 — **The Environment and World History**
XXVII, 3, 2004 — **Russia and Siberia in the World-
System: German Perspectives**
XXVII, 1, 2004 — **Directions for World-Systems
Analysis?**
XXVI, 2, 2003 — **Ecology of the Modern World-System**
XXV, 3, 2002 — **Utopian Thinking**
XXIV, 1, 2001 — **Braudel and the U.S.:** *Interlocuteurs
valables?*
XXIII, 4, 2000 — **Development Revisited**
XXIII, 1, 2000 — **Commodity Chains in the World-
Economy, 1590–1790**
XXII, 4, 1999 — **Caribbean Migrants to Core Zones**
XXII, 3, 1999 — **ReOrientalism?**
XXI, 3 & 4, 1998 — **The States, the Markets, and the
Societies: Separate Logics or a Single
Domain?**
XX, 3/4, Sum./Fall, 1997 — **Nomothetic vs. Idiographic
Disciplines: A False Dilemma?**

A brochure containing the Table of Contents of past issues is available on request.

Institutions $98/yr.
Individuals $28/yr.
Non-U.S. addresses,
postage $8/yr.
Special rate for low gnp
per capita countries $10/yr.

Managing Editor, *Review*
Fernand Braudel Center
Binghamton University
State University of New York
PO Box 6000
Binghamton, NY 13902-6000

boundary 2

Duke University Press presents

Critical Secularism

a special issue of *boundary 2*

Volume 31 Number 2

Aamir R. Mufti, special issue editor

At a moment in history when the world seems increasingly drawn into a violent "clash of fundamentalisms," this *boundary 2* special issue brings together renowned figures in cultural studies and literary theory to rethink critically the narratives of secularization that characterize modern culture.

SUBSCRIPTION INFORMATION

Three issues annually

Individuals: $33

Students: $20 (photocopy of valid student ID required)

Single issues: $14

Canadian orders:
Please include 7% GST and $9 postage.
Orders outside the U.S. and Canada:
Please include $12 postage.

To place your order using a credit card,
call toll-free 888-651-0122 (in the U.S. and Canada)
or 919-688-5134; or e-mail
subscriptions@dukeupress.edu.

For more information, please visit
www.dukeupress.edu/boundary2.

Contributors

Emily Apter

Akeel Bilgrami

Bishnupriya Ghosh

Willi Goetschel

Stathis Gourgouris

Gil Z. Hochberg

Ronald A. T. Judy

Aamir R. Mufti

Edward W. Said

Gayatri Chakravorty Spivak